David VanDrunen is one of the [...]
Reformed thinkers about the Ch[...]
he has put his pastoral application of that incisiveness into
print so that we might all benefit from his preaching through
Psalm 119. This great Psalm often feels daunting, but here we
have a master guide through its teaching on living the ups
and downs of repentance, confidence, emotion, sorrow, zeal,
and much more. As we sojourn this age of exile, VanDrunen
shows us the great hope of pilgriming through it with Christ
as our Shepherd.

Harrison Perkins
Pastor, Oakland Hills Community Church (OPC),
Farmington Hills, Michigan

Throughout Christian history, countless expositions and
commentaries have been written on the Psalms, yet there
are relatively few works that focus exclusively on Psalm 119.
Faith in Exile is one such volume, a simultaneously practical,
experiential, and spiritual exposition on Psalm 119. This
volume serves as a living testimony to the power of God's Word,
demonstrating how it sustains and strengthens Christians
who, like exiles, live in a world captive to sin and swept away
by waves of iniquity. Professor VanDrunen transcends mere
academic pursuits, offering scholarly depth, spiritual insight,
and the essence of experiential preaching to equip ministers of
the Word in both their pastoral ministry and daily lives. I pray
that no one neglects such a precious resource out of ignorance.

Changwon Shu
Professor, Chongshin Theological Seminary,
Seoul, South Korea

Psalm 119 is packed with timeless truths that for millennia have enlightened the paths of many pilgrims. VanDrunen explains these truths afresh with exegetical precision and practical application. These twelve contemporary sermons will help you meditate again upon God's law and thus be guided by the lamp of His truth through this present age.

Brian A. DeVries
Principal, Mukhanyo Theological College,
Pretoria, South Africa

Psalm 119 is the prayer of a sojourner, and, like the psalmist, we all live as pilgrims and strangers in a foreign land. Though we belong to God's covenant people, we may find ourselves sighing under oppression, persecution, and affliction in this world, making us acutely aware of our own frailty and lowliness. Among all the chapters of Scripture, none emphasizes the Word of God more frequently or intensely than Psalm 119, and it is fitting that a servant of the Word such as VanDrunen should write on this psalm.

Joonbum Kim
Senior Pastor, Yanguimoon Presbyterian Church,
Seoul, South Korea

Psalm 119 is a majestic Psalm that calls the reader to meditate on God's Word and delight in it, which makes Dave VanDrunen's book a fitting response. He serves as a careful, honest, and clear guide to exploring the richness of the Psalm and what obedience to it means for the Christian. Here are twelve edifying sermons that will benefit any Christian earnestly desiring to treasure God's Word.

Chase R. Kuhn
Rector, St Matthias Centennial Park, Sydney, Australia

FAITH IN EXILE

PSALM 119 & THE CHRISTIAN LIFE

DAVID VANDRUNEN

CHRISTIAN
FOCUS

print ISBN 978-1-5271-1254-4

ebook ISBN 978-1-5271-1327-5

10 9 8 7 6 5 4 3 2 1

Published in 2025

by

Christian Focus Publications Ltd.,

Geanies House, Fearn, Ross-shire

IV20 1TW, Great Britain.

www.christianfocus.com

Cover design by Rhian Muir

Printed and bound by
Bell and Bain Glasgow

MIX

Paper | Supporting responsible forestry

FSC

FSC® C007785

www.fsc.org

Contents

Preface

When I first began preaching Psalm 119 in late 2019, I had no anticipation of turning sermons into a book. Although I preach in many different churches rather than from a single pulpit, I ordinarily preach series from a book of Scripture. Even if congregations do not hear the whole series, at least it is helpful for me to preach in this way. I began preaching in Psalm 119 for two basic reasons. The first was that I was beginning work on a big project that would include an extended study of God's law, and spending some focused time on Psalm 119 was obviously relevant for that study. The second was that although I had read Psalm 119 countless times I had never felt that the psalm, as a whole, had really clicked in my mind. I had pondered how particular stanzas fit together, with partial satisfaction, but I was not clear at all on how the psalm cohered as a whole. Doing some preaching on the Long Psalm would be a good occasion, I hoped, to gain some greater clarity on this issue.

I had no commitment to preach through the entire psalm, and I did not know at the time how far I would get. As it turned out, I preached through all of Psalm 119, taking two stanzas at a time. I enjoyed doing so immensely and learned a great deal along the way. Still, presenting these sermons in a book was not at all an obvious thing to do. I have written and edited many books, but never one like this. Two strong considerations argued against it, in my mind.

The first is the nature of preaching itself, at least from my perspective. Preaching is a mode of oral communication in which a preacher ordained by Christ through his church proclaims God's word to his assembled covenant people, especially on the Lord's Day. Oral communication is simply not the same as written communication. The dynamic encounter between God's preached word and his assembled people is different from sitting in a chair and reading. In a sermon, a preacher who has researched, reflected, and prayed over a text of Scripture opens his heart to the hearts of the congregation. If that is the case, any sermon reduced to the written word loses something important. This loss seemed all the more substantial to me since I do not write my sermons in a manuscript but preach them from a fairly brief outline. In short, I am somewhat skeptical about *reading* sermons in the first place, and in any case I had no written sermons on Psalm 119 to work with.

The second consideration against turning my sermons on Psalm 119 into a book was the fact that I have no illusions that these sermons are somehow among the upper echelon of sermons preached and thus ought to be distributed more broadly than to the often-small congregations to which I preached them. I gave considerable thought to these sermons, but working on Psalm 119 was never my primary endeavor in life. I prepared and preached these sermons amidst many other responsibilities, some of which demanded much more of my time and energy than Psalm 119 did.

And yet the fact that you are reading this means that I have turned these sermons into a short book, despite these obstacles. With respect to my second hesitation above, perhaps the best

I can say is that I thoroughly enjoyed working through Psalm 119, learned a great deal, was blessed by it, and find some satisfaction in sharing what I have learned with others. As I preached these texts in dozens of churches, I heard many stories about how ordinary Christians read and study Psalm 119. People I did not know approached me after services and told me that they read and meditate on a verse in Psalm 119 every morning. Others have told me about Bible studies in which they explored all the terms for God's word that Psalm 119 uses. One person told me about how he memorized (almost) the whole of Psalm 119 while in prison. Many Christians love Psalm 119 and want to learn more about it.

And this leads to a second reason why I decided to turn these sermons into a book: there does not seem to be a crowded field of thorough studies of Psalm 119 that treat the Great Psalm as a coherent, logically organized, Christ-centered poem written by a godly and brilliant poet who adhered to a thoroughly old covenant religious faith yet eagerly expected the greater things of the new covenant and new creation. There are older collections of sermons on Psalm 119, some much longer than the present volume, but they tend to treat Psalm 119 as 176 individual pious statements rather than as a single, interconnected poem. Expounding Psalm 119 in this way can undoubtedly be edifying, but it is not the way my sermons treat Psalm 119, nor do I think it is the best way to treat it. Furthermore, the past several years have afforded me numerous opportunities to talk to pastors about Psalm 119, and although many have told me that they have preached a few stanzas of Psalm 119 or aspire to preach the psalm someday, I cannot recall any pastor telling me that he had preached through the whole of the psalm. So, perhaps the sermons in this volume can provide a resource that is not abundantly available. They may be able to help ordinary Bible-loving Christians who like studying Psalm 119 and want to learn more, and they may be able to stimulate pastors who would like to preach Psalm 119 but have not been sure how to do so. I want to be clear that I would not expect any pastor to preach these texts in the same way I have. But if my sermons can provide any motivation or insight for preaching Psalm 119, I would be very grateful for that.

With respect to my first hesitation described above, there is ultimately no way around the fact that hearing a sermon in the assembly of God's covenant people is not the same as reading a book, even if precisely the same words are spoken/written in each case. But there is a long Christian tradition of preserving and distributing sermons in written form, and just because two things are not the same does not mean both cannot be edifying. In creating this book, I have tried to be generally faithful to the words I spoke in particular sermons, to the degree that seemed possible and readable. I used an automated transcription service to provide transcripts of sermons recorded by churches where I preached. I then edited these transcripts. In part, I had to edit the mistakes in the transcript. For example, the first letter in the Hebrew alphabet is Aleph, not Olive, as some transcriptions thought, and I often referred to "our psalmist" but never to "Osama." I also tried to delete quirks and to smooth out rough spots that I suppose are inevitable in oral communication when one is speaking extemporaneously rather than reading a manuscript. But the following chapters are close to my real-life sermons.

I also resisted the temptation to improve the earlier sermons in light of what I learned as I worked my way through subsequent stanzas of Psalm 119. Perhaps I could have made these sermons a bit better, but I did not for two main reasons. For one thing, if I was going to produce this book, I wanted to fill it with real sermons, along the lines of what I wrote just above. If I tried to improve them by revising the transcripts, they would turn into something else. Moreover, it is a common experience for preachers to look back at sermons they preached at the beginning of a series, from the vantage point of the end of the series, and recognize certain deficiencies. How couldn't a preacher who studies and reflects seriously on a book of Scripture understand its first chapter better after preaching through the entire book than when he preached that first chapter months or years earlier? Sermons are not the sorts of things preachers endlessly tinker with. They preach sermons and move on. My decision not to try to improve the earlier sermons in light of the latter will give these sermons, I believe, a more authentic feel than would otherwise be the case, and I hope readers will appreciate that. As they read from earlier to later sermons, readers may perceive the development and maturing of my own thought about this psalm.

The final sermon in this book, however, is a recap of the entire psalm. In that sermon, I bring out some themes and emphases in earlier stanzas that were underdeveloped in the sermons that focused on those stanzas. When preaching that last sermon, I had a greater sense of what Psalm 119 as a whole is about than I had when I began preaching it.

Since what follow are sermons, I include no footnotes or other references to resources that have helped me along the way. So I mention two here for which I am especially grateful. Hywel Jones, my friend and former colleague at Westminster Seminary California, preached chapel sermons on Psalm 119 many years ago and subsequently wrote *Psalm 119 for Life* (Evangelical Press, 2009). I am thankful for how his sermons and book stimulated my thinking about the Great Psalm. Among academic resources, I found Will Soll's *Psalm 119: Matrix, Form, and Setting* (Catholic Biblical Association, 1991) to be especially helpful for understanding the themes of stanzas and the development of themes through the psalm as a whole.

I do not read sermons often, but I have been told that many authors of books of sermons tell readers that they have only published the sermons because people have urged them to do so for the good of the kingdom. No one urged me to publish these sermons for the good of the kingdom, so I cannot blame anyone else if readers find them unedifying. But I do thank my son, Jack, for giving me a good idea. I had originally toyed with writing a short book (from scratch) on what I learned about Psalm 119, but did not know how I would find time to do this in the near future given my many other commitments. Jack suggested that I simply publish the sermons. I decided that was indeed the best route, so I am grateful to him for suggesting it.

I am also thankful to the many churches who invited me to preach and listened to these sermons and received them graciously. I used recordings (without asking) from three congregations—Escondido Orthodox Presbyterian Church (Escondido, CA), Christ United Reformed Church (Anaheim, CA), and Westminster Orthodox Presbyterian Church (Westminster, CA)—and so I thank these churches too for their accessible and up-to-date sermon archives. Escondido OPC and the Reformed Presbyterian Church of Los Angeles were the only churches where I preached all twelve of these sermons. I am truly grateful for the mysterious fellowship that preacher and congregation enjoy in the ministry of God's word.

1

Holistic Obedience

Psalm 119:1-16

In the first major section of the Epistle to the Romans, from approximately the middle of chapter 1 to the middle of chapter 3, Paul laid the foundation for his great teaching on the doctrine of salvation by describing the sinfulness of the entire human race, Jew and Gentile alike. Amid that discussion, you may remember, Paul spoke about the Jewish people of his day. He said that they considered the law of Moses to be "the embodiment of knowledge and truth." In his larger argument in Romans 2, Paul exposed these people's sins. But he did not condemn them for thinking this about the law. He condemned them for not acting as though it is true. He condemned them for not obeying this law. They were right to view the law of God as the embodiment of knowledge and truth.

That is an interesting way to put it, isn't it? The *embodiment*— or the shape or form—of truth. This does not mean that the Mosaic law itself reveals all truth that can be known. But it does say that the law of Moses in some special and powerful way summed up the truth that God's people really needed to know.

Now we might wonder where the Jewish people of Paul's day got that idea. One very plausible answer to that question is Psalm 119.

Psalm 119 stands out. It is a well-known psalm for many reasons. One reason, of course, is because it is so long. There is a reason it is called the "Long Psalm" or the "Great Psalm." It is the single longest chapter in Scripture. Psalm 119 is also notable because it is an acrostic poem, which means that the Hebrew alphabet provides its structure. It has twenty-two stanzas, matching the Hebrew alphabet's twenty-two letters. Thus, in the first stanza, the first letter of every verse is the Hebrew letter Aleph, the first letter of that alphabet. In the second stanza, the first letter of every verse is the Hebrew letter Beth, the second letter of the alphabet. And so on.

But another interesting thing about this psalm is its focus upon God's law. Read the whole of Psalm 119—long as it is—and you will not find anything about Abraham, Isaac, and Jacob. You also will not find any mention of the exodus from Egypt, the covenants, the temple in Jerusalem, or the throne of David. Those are all important themes in the Old Testament, yet they do not appear in Psalm 119. Instead, Psalm 119 keeps talking about the law. This psalm has a stock of Hebrew terms for referring to the law that it uses over and over. Almost every verse uses one of these terms. The law of God certainly does shine forth as the embodiment of knowledge and truth in Psalm 119.

But please keep one thing in mind as you meditate on Psalm 119. We often think of "the law" merely as God's commandments, in distinction from "the gospel" which proclaims God's promises of salvation in Christ. That is indeed an important theological distinction. But "the law" can also refer to the opening section of Scripture—that is, the first five books of the Old Testament. And these books—Genesis through Deuteronomy—contain more than commandments. They also have stories of God's faithfulness, prophecies of God's future grace, and the like. This is why those terms that appear repeatedly in Psalm 119 include "way," "promise," and simply "word." "The law" in this sense reveals all sorts of "knowledge and truth," not just information about rules to obey.

We consider here the first two stanzas—Aleph and Beth. These opening stanzas teach that the law of God requires comprehensive obedience and a holistic devotion on the part of God's people. We look first at the opening stanza, verses 1-8.

* * * * *

Verses 1-2 raise a crucial question: How are God's people blessed? Notice how both verses begin: "Blessed are those…. Blessed are those…." These two consecutive verses begin in the same way. We do not find this elsewhere in Psalm 119. And nothing is more important than being blessed by God.

How do God's people receive blessing from their Lord? These opening verses provide a simple and clear answer. God's people are blessed through walking in the law of the Lord and by keeping his testimonies. That is, God's people are blessed by adhering to God's word.

Yet this straightforward answer needs some embellishment. In fact, verses 1-4 show that there is more to it than this. For one thing, these opening verses show that blessing comes not through obeying God's law in a vague or general sense but through a comprehensive and thorough obedience. We see this in each of the first four verses. Verse 1: "Blessed are those whose way is *blameless*." No blame at all. Verse 2: "Blessed are those…who seek him *with their whole heart*." Not with half their heart, but with all of it. Verse 3: "Who also do *no* wrong."

Not those who rarely do wrong, but who do no wrong at all. And then verse 4: God has commanded his "precepts to be kept *diligently*." Not with some effort, some of the time, but with diligence, all the time. If the psalmist made only one of these statements in passing it might be easy to overlook. But how striking and remarkable that the opening of this psalm bombards us with this emphasis upon the comprehensive, holistic obedience that the law requires for God's blessing.

So that is one thing to recognize in these opening verses. And here is a second thing: The law, as important as it is—as much as it demands thorough, comprehensive obedience—is not an end in itself. In verse 2, the psalmist says: "Blessed are those…who seek *him* with their whole heart." You see, we should obey the law because it points us to the Lord himself. We should obey the law as part of our broader quest to seek God. Many people who seem zealous for God's law fail to do this, and it is a great mistake. For them, the law takes on a life of its own. The law becomes its own great reward. But the law is only good and profitable for us if it leads us to know and serve the Lord sincerely.

These first four verses provide quite a striking opening to Psalm 119. And as we come to the second four verses—the second half of the Aleph stanza—we seem to come back down to earth a little. The first four verses set before us this great ideal of comprehensive obedience to God and his law but notice now in verses 5-8 how the psalmist's tone changes.

The psalmist begins verse 5 by saying: "Oh, that my ways may be steadfast." Here the psalmist *prays*. It is the first prayer in Psalm 119. I put it that way because, in a sense, the whole of Psalm 119 is a single long prayer. But within this great prayer we have many short, individual prayers. Some of the verses are not prayers, strictly speaking, but statements. But here in verse 5 we find the first little prayer: "Oh, that my ways may be steadfast in keeping your statutes." This prayer alerts us to something important. We do not usually ask for what we already have. We ask for what we need or want. The psalmist asks for steadfastness. He understands that he needs help. He is not as fully steadfast as he ought to be. He acknowledges his limits and his weakness.

Next, in verse 6, the psalmist says: "Then I shall not be put to shame, having my eyes fixed on all your commandments." "Put to shame" has a negative connotation. Yet it is understandable that the psalmist's mind turns in this direction. He began the psalm by reflecting on God's blessing. God's blessing comes through comprehensive obedience. But he must pray for steadfastness because he obviously sees some weakness in his own life. And that makes us wonder: If blessing comes through comprehensive obedience, what if we are not as steadfast as we ought to be? What if we are not comprehensively faithful in the ways of the Lord? If blessing comes through obedience, it implies that curse, judgment, and therefore *shame* will come through disobedience. So we see here in verses 5-6 that the psalmist's mind turns in a darker direction. His words make us wonder whether God's people can experience the blessing that he announced in verses 1-2.

Now, to be sure, verses 5-8 still have an overall positive focus. The psalmist does say that if God grants steadfastness he *will not* be put to shame. In verse 7 he says he will praise God as he learns his righteous rules. In verse 8 he says that he will keep his statutes. He commits himself to follow God's law, yet certain thoughts trouble us. If God's law really demands the kind of comprehensive obedience that verses 1-4 describe, and if the psalmist is not fully steadfast, how will he avoid the shame that disobedience to the law brings? And the end of the stanza—the last phrase of verse 8—enhances our uneasiness. The psalmist closes the first stanza by saying: "do not utterly forsake me." We wonder if he is already feeling forsaken by God and already experiencing God's displeasure Why else would he ask not to be *utterly* forsaken?

Now, we do not know who wrote this psalm. A long Christian tradition assumes that it was written by King David, who was of course a great psalmist. But we do not know that it was David, and in fact some parts of the psalm suggest that it was written later than David's day. Yet some features of Psalm 119 suggest that a king of Israel, someone in the line of David, may have written it. And that might make us yet more uneasy as we read this opening stanza: If this was a king of Israel and he was concerned about his own lack of steadfastness and about falling into shame because of disobedience, then what about the people of Israel as a whole? Often in the Old Testament the whole people of God suffered when the king was unfaithful.

A tension is brewing as we reach the end of the first stanza. We are not even 5 percent through this psalm and already a tension emerges that in a way is never resolved through the entirety of Psalm 119. The psalmist expresses his zeal for God's law throughout this psalm. He loves God's law. He commits himself to following it diligently. Yet at the same time he expresses this constant realization that comprehensive obedience eludes him. It is always outside of his grasp. He is a sinner.

Many things in Psalm 119 sound like the second part of Romans 7. That text expresses the mind and heart of someone who loves God's law and desires to do it and yet finds that he cannot. But one thing that is so beautiful about Romans 7 is the way it ends. "Who will deliver me from this body of death?" Paul asks (7:24). "Thanks be to God through our Lord Jesus Christ!" (7:25). Paul announced an answer to this great tension and uneasiness of those who love God's law but find themselves constantly falling short of its high demands.

But the fact is, we do not find such a clear answer presented in Psalm 119. Consider for a moment the very last verse of the psalm—verse 176. The psalm ends by saying: "I have gone astray like a lost sheep; seek your servant, for I do not forget your commandments." The psalm does not end with a ringing resolution to spiritual uneasiness. It ends with the psalmist's confession that he is a lost sheep and needs God to come and find him.

* * * * *

So we have come to the end of this first stanza and now proceed to the second. We find that the psalmist doubles down on this idea that the law requires perfect obedience. But he does so from a different angle. He now focuses on what holistic devotion looks like in a person who obeys God's law.

This Beth stanza begins in verse 9: "How can a young man keep his way pure? By guarding it according to your word." Why does the psalmist begin by talking about the young person? Perhaps one reason is to communicate already the holistic nature of devotion to God's law. Devotion to God's law should not begin when you become an adult. It is not a project for middle age or something wise to take up before you die. *From our youth* we ought to guard our way by following God's word. You who are young have less experience and less wisdom. You are even more vulnerable to the world's attractions and Satan's lies. Even from your youth you need to be committed to the law of God.

Then, in verses 10-11, the psalmist's attention turns back to the heart. Recall that in verse 2 he spoke of seeking God with the whole heart, and he revisits this theme in the second verse of the second stanza. Verse 10: "With my whole heart I seek you; let me not wander from your commandments!" Verse 11 makes this more concrete: "I have stored up your word in my heart, that I might not sin against you." To seek God wholeheartedly involves treasuring that word in our heart. What is the heart? In Scripture, the heart usually does not refer to the organ beating in our chest. The heart refers to our inmost character, to who we really are. Look at your heart if you want to know who you are deep down and what is truly valuable to you. The righteous person is the one who treasures the word of God and stores it up in his heart. What is precious to this person is the word of God. Many other places in Scripture echo these ideas. Proverbs 4 says that the heart is the wellspring of life. In Matthew 15, Jesus says that all sorts of sin spring forth from the heart. The heart is what makes you who you are. It reveals who you are. The righteous person's heart stores up the word of God.

After saying this, the psalmist presents a bit of an interlude in verse 12: "Blessed are you, O LORD; teach me your statutes." He pauses to bless God. This should remind us of some things we considered earlier. The law ultimately points to God. *God* is the one who is supremely important, not the law in and of itself. Here in verse 12 the psalmist also asks God to teach him his statutes. He again acknowledges his need. He is not self-sufficient to understand and keep God's law.

After this interlude, we come to the final four verses of the second stanza. The psalmist returns to his theme of holistic devotion. So think about this. Verse 9 says the law should be kept throughout one's entire life, even from one's youth. In verses 10-11, the word is held and guarded in one's heart, that is, in one's inmost being. And now, in verse 13, the psalmist moves from the inside to the outside, as it were: "With my lips I declare all the rules of your mouth." What is in the heart should be expressed on the lips. What is inside must be expressed on the outside. This is true, isn't it? Though we can fool people for a while by what we say, we cannot conceal what is inside us forever. What we say with our lips tends to express what is in our hearts—often to our embarrassment. We find this theme elsewhere in Scripture. You might think of Romans 10:9. Paul says that the person who confesses with his mouth that Jesus is Lord and believes in his heart that God raised him from the dead will be saved. What is in the heart should be expressed on the lips, and that is what the psalmist communicates here in verse 13: We declare the rules (or judgments) of God's mouth.

Then in verse 14 the psalmist moves back inward: "In the way of your testimonies I delight as much as in all riches." After speaking about what goes out from the lips, the psalmist describes again what he delights in. That gets back to the heart, to the core of our being. We should delight in God's law as much as we delight in riches. If I told you that you were going to receive a huge monetary windfall, would any of you not find that a happy thought? The psalmist says that, even as we instinctively delight in a large financial gift, the righteous person instinctively delights in the testimonies of God.

In verse 15, the psalmist moves back again from the inside to the outside: "I will meditate on your precepts"—which is internal—and then affirms, "[I will] fix my eyes on your ways." We express devotion to God's word not only with our lips but also with our eyes. A similar dynamic is at work. Even as what is in our heart tends to express itself with our lips, so also what is in our heart tends to express itself with our eyes. Sometimes we use the expression that we have our eye on this or that. We could mean that metaphorically to indicate something we want. But we can also use that expression quite literally. It is hard not to gaze at the objects of our obsession. Too often we set our sights on people we envy or lust after, or on things we covet. The eyes reflect what is in the heart. The righteous person has eyes fixed on God's ways.

Then in verse 16, the final verse, the psalmist again moves back inward, toward the heart: "I will delight in your statutes; I will not forget your word." The psalmist delights in God's statutes so much that he does not forget God's law. That is a remarkable thing, because it is easy to be forgetful. It gets easier as you get older! But we also know that some things are hard to forget. Sometimes we wish we could forget things but cannot. What is hard to forget? Things that are important to us. It is all too easy to forget what does not matter much. This is why it is so embarrassing when we forget things our spouses or children tell us. If we really care about something, we tend to remember it. The psalmist says, "I will delight in your statutes; I will not forget your word." The law of God should be so important to us that we do not forget it.

You can see that the psalmist has presented this holistic devotion to God's law very artfully in this second stanza. This devotion encompasses our heart, our eyes, our delight, our memory, our lips. Every single part of us should be devoted to the law of God.

* * * * *

As we come to the end of these two stanzas, how can we not be amazed by the utter comprehensiveness of the law's requirements and of the holistic devotion of the person who follows it? And although the psalmist does not develop this theme in detail yet, he does provide clues about his own weakness, helplessness, and failures as he seeks to obey God's law in this way. Already in the opening stanza the psalmist recognizes the danger of God's judgment and his own shame.

As we reflect on this psalm, we do so with the answer that Paul provided at the end of Romans 7: "Thanks be to God, through our Lord Jesus Christ!" It was the answer our psalmist was looking forward to but could not explain clearly and explicitly. He longed for it without identifying it. But we have the great privilege of reading this psalm in light of our knowledge of the Lord Jesus Christ's finished work.

As we do, nothing is more fitting than to reflect on the absolute, comprehensive obedience of the Lord Jesus. This doctrine is familiar to many of us. We confess that our Lord Jesus Christ was perfect, without sin. But how often do we reflect deeply on what that means? The very idea of perfection eludes us, doesn't it? Who of us can even begin to comprehend the experience of being utterly devoted to God with every single part of our being, at every single moment of our entire lives? We may have moments in life that provide a little glimpse of perfection—a bright student's 100 percent on a math quiz or the bowler who rolls a 300 game. Yet, ultimately, those things do not matter much. We can hardly compare them to a lifetime of absolute, comprehensive devotion to God's law.

Yet our Lord Jesus Christ had this absolute devotion. He had it even from his youth. Recall that wonderful story in Luke 2 when Jesus, as a boy, went to the temple of God. He amazed the teachers of the law because of his knowledge of God's word. Jesus was blameless. Through his entire life, no one could justly blame him for a single misdeed. He did nothing wrong. His heart always treasured God's law. On no occasion did he desire earthly riches more than he treasured God and his truth. And the Lord Jesus never once forgot. In thirty-some years of life, he never, ever forgot about God and his word. Yet, of course, he was forsaken on the cross. He was put to shame. He experienced the very things the psalmist feared.

As we think about such a Savior, we recognize one we can truly rely on. In Reformed churches, we talk a lot about the imputed righteousness of Christ: we stand justified before God's throne because Christ's righteousness has been credited to us. It is good that our pulpits proclaim this truth and that it becomes familiar to us. But do not let this become some sort of abstract doctrinal truth. You can stake your entire life on Christ's righteousness. This absolute, comprehensive obedience described in Psalm 119—it is yours. You claim this as your own when you rest on Christ. You have a Savior, at the right hand of the Father, who is looking out for you, praying for you, and guarding your hearts and minds. He is perfectly righteous. He is a Savior you can count on.

As we saw, Psalm 119 begins by declaring people blessed. Perhaps that reminds you of the Beatitudes, some of the first words we hear from the lips of Jesus in the New Testament. Among the blessed are those who hunger and thirst after righteousness. This describes us as Christians. As followers of the Lord Jesus Christ, we hunger and thirst after righteousness. Let us not forget though that a few verses later in Matthew 5, Jesus said: "Do not think that I have come to abolish the Law or the Prophets; I have not come to abolish them but to fulfill them." Jesus came to perform all the purposes and requirements of the law of God. May that Savior give us grace to hunger and thirst after his righteousness. May he give us the grace to love his ways. And may he give us that heart to admire and to trust such a beautiful, perfect, all-sufficient Savior.

2

A Sojourner on Earth

Psalm 119:17-32

In the first two stanzas of the Long Psalm, verses 1-16, we saw the psalmist meditating on the comprehensive obedience that God's law sets before his people and on the holistic devotion it requires from them—a devotion that springs from the heart and expresses itself through the mouth and with the eyes. But we also saw a certain uneasiness in these opening stanzas. A tension emerges early in the psalm. The psalmist dedicates himself to following this law wholeheartedly, yet he senses his desperate need for God's help. Because of his own weakness, he recognizes that shame is a very real danger when he contemplates the perfections of God's law.

As we come to the next two stanzas—Gimel and Daleth— we find more uneasiness and tension. Yet this uneasiness comes from a different place from where we saw it in the first two stanzas. In the stanzas before us now, the psalmist does not so much contemplate his own weakness or lack of steadfastness as he contemplates the fact that he is a sojourner on the earth.

He is an exile. He is living in a place far from his home in the Promised Land of Canaan. What is more, he is the object of other people's scorn and contempt, despite his devotion to God's law. These items should get our attention, for the New Testament teaches that we, as new covenant Christians, are sojourners and exiles too, not because we are banished from an earthly holy land but because we still live in this present evil age and have not yet reached the glory of the new creation. Psalm 119 surely has much to teach us about pursuing a godly life while sojourning.

As we saw in the previous text, so again here Psalm 119 does not provide a final answer to the uneasiness our psalmist feels. Yet even these verses before us point to God's gracious response. This psalmist calls, and God answers him. The psalmist anticipates the deliverance from a sinful world that we as New Testament believers have already begun to enjoy, even though our present earthly sojourn is filled with many trials.

* * * * *

We look first at the Gimel stanza, the third stanza of Psalm 119, verses 17-24. The stanza begins with a wonderful statement: "Deal bountifully with your servant that I may live and keep your word." What was the psalmist thinking of when he asked God to "deal bountifully" with him? He might have been looking back and considering times when God had dealt bountifully with his people. He might have thought back to creation, when God set our first parents in a garden that overflowed with bounty—with good food, precious metals, and abundant waters. Or perhaps he was remembering when God brought his people Israel through the wilderness and into the Promised Land. Think about how bountifully God dealt with his people then, giving them a prosperous land flowing with milk and honey. The psalmist knew that God had dealt bountifully with his people in the past. And he adds here: Deal bountifully with your servant "that I may *live* and keep your word." At those earlier times in history—in the Garden of Eden and when God brought Israel into the Promised Land—God set life before his people. He set the tree of life before them in paradise, and he offered them long life in the Promised Land. And on both occasions he called his people to keep his word. It is understandable, in that light, that in the next verse— verse 18—the psalmist says: "Open my eyes that I may behold wondrous things out of your law." As he thinks about the bounty with which God had dealt with his people, he expects to see wondrous things out of God's word even in his own day.

This is an upbeat, positive opening to the stanza. But note how drastically the mood changes when we come to verse 19. The psalmist says: "I am a sojourner on the earth." A sojourner is a person on the move. He is not settled in one place. Sojourners travel in places that are not their true home, in places they do not really belong.

As we reflect on sojourning in the Scriptures, we might think back to Abraham. On many occasions, Genesis recounts that Abraham and his family *sojourned* here or there. Abraham moved around from place to place. He lived in tents. He never really settled. In his lifetime he never obtained the inheritance God had promised him. And as I mentioned earlier, we new covenant believers are sojourners too. First Peter 2:11, for example, calls us "sojourners and exiles." This makes sense of our present identity. The New Testament tells us that our citizenship is in heaven. That is where we really belong. That is our place of ultimate allegiance. Yet here we are, still on earth. Here we are, in this present evil age. Even if you have lived in the same place for your whole life, as a Christian you are a sojourner because you are still traveling, as it were. You are away from where your true home is.

When our psalmist says, "I am a sojourner," it is crucial to recognize that something is wrong. This was not the way it was supposed to be for our psalmist. He was an Israelite living under the law of Moses. He was living after the time of Abraham and before Christ brought in the new covenant. And Israelites under Moses were not supposed to be sojourners. In an important sense, they were to be settled. God had given them a Promised Land, a good land in which to enjoy peace, prosperity, and victory over their enemies. They were not to be traveling around. But here the psalmist says: "I am a sojourner."

What is he saying about his condition? It is theoretically possible that he is still in the land of Israel but is on the run from someone. Most likely, he has been driven out of the land and is in exile, perhaps in the Babylonian exile. Whatever exactly the psalmist's situation, something is not right. In fact, the Mosaic law had told Israel that if they were disobedient and went after other gods, God would exile them from their land as punishment. This background should impress upon us just how ominous the psalmist's description of himself is.

And there is more. In the second part of verse 19 the psalmist prays: "Hide not your commandments from me." As he endures this time of sojourning, God's revelation is hidden from his eyes. He cannot see it clearly. It is obscure to him. He needs God to make his word clear to him again. Yet in verse 20, even in his terrible condition, he says: "My soul is consumed with longing for your rules at all times." He does not cease to desire God's word. He longs for it, and that longing consumes him. But we get the sense that this longing was not exactly satisfied.

The psalmist then finishes this third stanza, in verses 21-23, by elaborating on his experience as sojourner. He does not merely mention that he is a sojourner and move on to something else. No, he helps us understand the nature of his condition. Verse 21 describes the way things are supposed to work: "You rebuke the insolent, accursed ones, who wander from your commandments." Yes, exactly right. The law of Moses says repeatedly that God will rebuke those who wander from his law. Those insolent, proud people stand under God's condemnation. That is how it is supposed to be.

But look at how the psalmist comments on his own condition in the next two verses. Verse 22: "Take away from me scorn and contempt, for I have kept your testimonies." He is enduring scorn. He is the victim of contempt. Yet he describes himself as a man who keeps God's testimonies. He is devoted to God's law, but he endures the contempt that the godless deserve. That does *not* seem like the way things are supposed to be. As if that is not enough, verse 23 adds: "Even though princes sit plotting against me, your servant will meditate on your statutes." Princes were plotting against him! As I mentioned in the previous chapter, we cannot know with certainty who wrote this psalm. But some clues hint that its author was an Israelite king, a descendant of David and heir to his throne. And if that is the case, how terrible verse 23 is! According to the Mosaic law, when Israelite rulers were faithful to God's law, they would conquer other kings. Yet our psalmist says that princes are plotting against him. *He* is on the receiving end. *He* is the victim. Matters seem flipped on their head. He is a sojourner. He adds in verse 24, however, "Your testimonies are my delight; they are my counselors." He does not cease to look to God and his law, even though everything seems out of order.

As we come to the end of this stanza, let us reflect on it as a whole. According to the law of Moses, obedience to God should have brought Israel prosperity, peace, and rest in their Promised Land. The law indicated that those who were obedient and devoted to God would flourish. God would bless them and give them victory over their enemies. But those who disobeyed and disregarded God's law in pride would suffer. They would endure scorn, contempt, and shame. So what has happened with our psalmist? How can he delight in God's word and yet suffer the curse of the wicked? Was he still suffering for past sins from which he has now repented? Or was he among the faithful remnant during a time of widespread rebellion in Israel, such that he is suffering on account of others' unrighteousness? Or perhaps there simply was no easy explanation for our psalmist's condition. After all, God's ways with Israel were not always crystal clear. That was especially true at times when God's people were, or believed themselves to be, generally devoted to God and yet suffered, nonetheless. Sometimes they felt the weight of God's curse upon them from those who were far more wicked than they were. Situations like this were very difficult and at times even provoked a crisis of faith for God's people of old. Consider Psalm 44. That psalmist cried out that God had forsaken Israel. God was not going out to battle with Israel, even though Israel had not forsaken God. What was going on? How to understand this? The author of Psalm 44 did not have an answer. Perhaps the author of Psalm 119 had similar questions and also no answer.

We will have to leave these matters open for now. Our psalmist does in fact provide more insight on the issues, but we must keep reading the rest of this Long Psalm to find it. Rather than laying out all his insights from the outset, the psalmist requires us to be patient as he takes us through his spiritual experience. But already the next stanza helps us to understand him better. And it also helps us to learn from Psalm 119 as new covenant Christians who also often struggle to understand our experience as sojourners in this world.

* * * * *

We turn to the fourth stanza, Daleth, verses 25-32. This stanza begins in verse 25 on the same train of thought on which the psalmist concluded the previous stanza: "My soul clings to the dust." He is still weighed down by the curse of this world and by the contempt of God's enemies. In fact, he makes a similar statement shortly thereafter, in verse 28: "My soul melts away for sorrow; strengthen me according to your word." The psalmist begins this new stanza still feeling the burdens of life as a sojourner.

But consider verses 26-27, the verses in between the two verses I just mentioned. These statements provide a wonderful response to the psalmist's uneasiness and tension—an antidote, perhaps, to a potential crisis of faith: "When I told of my ways, you answered me; teach me your statutes. Make me understand the way of your precepts, and I will meditate on your wondrous works." Notice the beginning of verse 26: he tells God of his ways. His "ways" are likely the ways he has been telling us about in the previous stanza: that of striving after God's law and nevertheless sojourning, suffering contempt, and suffering opposition from princes. He tells these things to God. He does not hide them, but lays bare his soul to the Lord. And he adds: "You answered me." The Lord was not silent. The Lord is not deaf to his people when they open their hearts to him. The Lord answers. And the psalmist says in the next verse, verse 27, "Make me understand the way of your precepts, and I will meditate on your wondrous works." The psalmist could surely think back on a multitude of wondrous works God had done, even at this point in redemptive history. He had brought Israel out of Egypt and into the Promised Land, for instance. The psalmist could think back on these and be confident that God would do yet more wondrous things in response to his people's prayers. The psalmist displays great faith here. And notice something else in verses 26 and 27. In verse 26 he tells of his "*ways*," and then in verse 27 he says: "Make me understand the *way* of your precepts." He recounted *his own* ways, but now he expresses desire to follow *God's* ways. He wants his own ways to conform to God's.

We wonder, of course, what exactly the answer was which God gave our psalmist. The psalmist does not tell us. Yet we do know that the Mosaic law—a great focus of Psalm 119—promised that when God's people were in distress and cried out to him, he would answer and restore them. Even if they sinned and suffered his wrath, he would not abandon his commitment to his people. For example, Deuteronomy 30 prophesied that Israel would disobey the law and God would scatter them among the nations—that is, make them sojourners. But in Deuteronomy 30 God also promised that when this happened, even when they were at their lowest point, he would renew his grace and restore them. To use our psalmist's language, he would do a wondrous new work among them. Surely our psalmist was clinging to such promises.

In light of this, we can hardly be surprised that when we turn to the second half of this Daleth stanza, verses 29-32, we find quite a positive tone. Much that we have considered thus far in our text has been sobering rather than positive. Yet in these final verses our psalmist's spirit rises again in confidence before God. Notice some of the things he says. In verses 29-30 he returns to the theme of the "way" that we saw in verses 26-27. There he reflected on his own ways and then turned to God's way, that is, the way of God's law. Here, in verse 29, he says (in my own translation), "Put the way of falsehood far from me," and in verse 30: "I have chosen the way of faithfulness." He turns away from the way of *falsehood* and he strives after the way of *faithfulness*. He has chosen God's way rather than the deceptive way of human sin. Then in verse 31 he says: "I cling to your testimonies, O LORD." Do you remember what he wrote in verse 25? "My soul clings to the dust." He is still clinging, but now not to the dust but to God's testimonies. The psalmist uses his poetic skills to describe this transformation in his spiritual condition.

Finally, we come to verse 32, and what a conclusion to the stanza! He says: "I will run in the way of your commandments." You might remember from verse 1: "Blessed are those who walk in the law of the LORD." *Walking* in the way of the Lord sounded good at the time, didn't it? But how much better to *run* in the way of the Lord! This indicates strength and endurance. And the psalmist concludes by saying that he will run in the way of God's commandments "when you enlarge my heart." That is an interesting statement. If you are going to run an earthly race, it really helps to have a strong, healthy heart. Here our psalmist looks forward to having a strong spiritual heart. Of course, God did strengthen the hearts of his old covenant people. But keep in mind those Old Testament promises about how God would deal with people in the last days, after Christ's coming. Some great prophecies of the new covenant promised even greater blessing for the hearts of God's people. Consider Ezekiel 36, where God promised them a new heart and a new spirit. Or consider Jeremiah 31, the most famous prophecy of the new covenant, where God said he would write the law on the hearts of his people. Perhaps our psalmist was clinging to such promises. O LORD, "I will run in the way of your commandments when you enlarge my heart!" What a wonderful way for this stanza to end.

* * * * *

We have come to the end of our text. As we have moved from the first stanza to the second, third, and fourth, the number of petitions increases. The psalmist keeps asking God for more things, more frequently. In the first stanza, he asked for two things. He asked for two things also in the second stanza. In the third stanza, he asks for four things. And in this fourth stanza, he asks for six things. He continues to meditate upon the perfections of God's law, his own weakness, and his own difficult circumstances, and this compels him to pray more. He multiplies his cries to God for help. The more he reflects, the more he knows he needs the mercy of his God. But as he multiplies his petitions he also says in faith: "You answered me." And the psalmist, in light of God's answer, turns from his own ways to God's ways. He turns from the way of falsehood to the way of faithfulness. He looks forward to running in this way with an enlarged heart.

If you keep reading Psalm 119, you will find plenty more that is discouraging, sobering, and puzzling. But the end of this Daleth stanza is a relative high point in which the psalmist anticipates God's great answer to his people's distress. He could see this answer in part already, but he also expected God to give it more fully in later days.

God has now given that greater answer to us, New Testament Christians, by sending his Son and establishing a new and better covenant. This answer was surely not exactly what our psalmist expected it to be. For one thing, God's answer in these last days has not made his people more devoted to the law of Moses as such. In fact, Christ came under that law to redeem us from it. He came to deliver us from its curse upon sinners and to give us something much better than its types and shadows. What is more, God's answer to his people's pleas of old has not made us something other than sojourners. The psalmist struggled with life as a sojourner because he experienced it as a curse of the Mosaic law. But God has made his new covenant people sojourners of a different kind. We, the church of Jesus Christ, are not scattered in this world longing to return to an earthly promised land. No, Christ has already made us citizens of his heavenly kingdom. We are sojourners because we are not yet in glory. But praise God that it is not a curse for us to be sojourners in the world here and now. God is not punishing us for breaking the new covenant. Being sojourners in a fallen, evil world is difficult. It brings many spiritual trials. But we can endure our present sojourn without needing to wonder whether God has forsaken us or is angry with us. We wait patiently for Christ to return, with great confidence that we are right with God by faith and that he keeps our heavenly inheritance firm and secure until that day.

Thus, even now we have strength to run in the ways of the Lord. Think about the end of Isaiah 40, one of the great, majestic chapters of Scripture. There the prophet was also preparing the old covenant people for deliverance from their exile and for the coming of the blessings of the new covenant. As the prophet came to the end of that great chapter, he spoke of a time when the Lord would renew his people's strength. They would soar on wings as eagles. They would run and not be weary, walk and not faint. This is the strength the Lord has already begun to pour out upon his people in these last days.

And what about an enlarged heart? Because Christ has established the new covenant, Hebrews 8 makes clear that the promise of Jeremiah 31 stands fulfilled. God has written his law upon your hearts. The Lord has enlarged your hearts and poured out his Spirit in yet more abundant measure than what this psalmist ever experienced.

Still, the Lord has not yet taken away our call to be sojourners in this world. We are travelers. We are away from our true home. And it is not easy. We feel the shame, scorn, and contempt of God's enemies. We are never sure what is going to come next in this world. We fear princes who would rise up against us and persecute us for our faith. Yet the Lord comes to us under the new covenant and assures us that our time of sojourning is not a curse. Suffering does not mean that you are under God's displeasure or that you have done something wrong. Amid our sojourn, the Lord promises never to leave us or forsake us. He makes us more than conquerors in him who loved us. And he gives us strength to turn to him day by day and to know that he works out all things for the good of those who love him, who are called according to his purpose.

Take heart that you will not be sojourners forever. You are citizens of heaven now and one day you will be residents too. You walk by faith now but soon you will walk by sight. May that be a great encouragement to you today and—as the old hymn put it—"till trav'ling days are done."

3

Lifting Up Hands in Uneasy Times

Psalm 119:33-48

We consider this text under unusual circumstances, to say the least.[1] Surely none of us can honestly say that we feel no anxiety, fear, tension, or uneasiness. Our hearts feel deeply the uncertainties of this time.

I did not choose the text before us for this occasion especially but am simply continuing to preach through Psalm 119. Yet in certain respects Psalm 119 is a very appropriate psalm for us to consider. If for no other reason, the psalmist who wrote this was suffering his own uneasiness. This psalmist was not in a good place, as we might say. The psalmist was not feeling confident about his affairs of the present life. This is a psalm that oozes uneasiness and tension and even uncertainty to some degree. As we come before the Lord and his word this day, we do so with uneasy hearts. We consider a psalm that breathes that very same experience.

The first two stanzas, Aleph and Beth, begin with great statements about God's law, about the perfect and holistic

---

1 I initially preached this sermon in March 2020, on the first Sunday after California imposed its first Covid lockdown. It was this congregation's first online service.

obedience that the law requires, and about the psalmist's desire to express such wholehearted obedience. Yet, from the very first stanza, we see the psalmist's uneasiness begin to break through. He prays that he would be steadfast. He is afraid that he might be put to shame. He is concerned that God might utterly forsake him. These concerns appear already in the first stanza.

Then, in the third and fourth stanzas, the psalmist reflects on the fact that he is a sojourner on earth. In some ways the psalmist is the opposite of those of us who were sheltering at home, as our civil authorities told us to do. We were trapped in our homes while the psalmist was trapped *away* from home. He was a sojourner. And since this psalmist was an Old Testament Israelite, that was a source of concern. The Israelites living under the law were not supposed to be sojourners. They were to be secure and blessed in their Promised Land as they obeyed God and his law. We cannot be sure who this psalmist was or in what period he wrote, but we know that he was away from home. Perhaps he was one of the Babylonian exiles. Whatever the case, this was not good. In the third stanza, Gimel, he said that he was the object of scorn and contempt and that princes were plotting against him. At the beginning of the fourth stanza, Daleth, he wrote: "My soul clings to the dust." This psalmist understood what it was to endure trouble and trial.

We find many of the same ideas in the fifth and sixth stanzas. The psalmist reflects on the goodness of God's law, he seeks to delight in obedience to it, and he expects some great work of God. Yet we also see the uneasiness, uncertainty, and tension that remains. Even as he looks in confidence to God, he does not know exactly how God is going to deliver him. But he knows that God will. So we turn now to the fifth stanza—the letter He.

* * * * *

The opening verses of the stanza begin by recapping previously expressed ideas. This is not unusual: several stanzas of Psalm 119 begin by recapping what came before. In the preceding stanza, Daleth, a key theme was how the psalmist forsook his former evil ways and was striving to follow God's way of faithfulness. He picks this up here at the beginning of He: "Teach me, O LORD, the way of your statutes; and I will keep it to the end." Then, a couple of verses later, he says: "Lead me in the path of your commandments, for I delight in it." So again he resolves to walk in the way and path of the Lord.

He also reflects on another theme that has been prominent thus far, especially in the second stanza. He asks in verse 34: "Give me understanding, that I may keep your law and observe it with my whole heart." It is not difficult to understand why the psalmist emphasizes *the heart*. Without wholehearted devotion internally, how is this psalmist going to walk externally in the way of the Lord? The psalmist again determines to be holistically obedient to the Lord, in both his inward heart and his walk in this world.

Yet we do not have to read far into this stanza to meet the uneasiness that the psalmist expresses throughout the psalm. For one thing, which is quite easy to miss if you are not looking for it, the psalmist offers a prayer to God in every single one of these eight verses. Each verse petitions God. As the psalm has progressed to this point, the number of petitions in each stanza increases. The first two stanzas have only two petitions. Then the third stanza increases to four petitions. By the fourth stanza the psalmist is up to six petitions. And here in the fifth stanza all eight verses lift a prayer to God. This is intentional. The psalmist is communicating something to us. The more he reflects on God's law, on his own heart, and on his situation in this world, he gains a greater and greater sense of his neediness before God. He cannot rescue himself. The Lord must act. The Lord must do a great work for him and in him.

This is one way the psalmist alerts us to the uneasiness he feels. But also, right in the center of this fifth stanza, the psalmist mentions things standing against him. In verse 36 he says: "Incline my heart to your testimonies, and not to selfish gain." He recognizes his own tendency toward self-centeredness. Then he says in the next verse: "Turn my eyes from looking at worthless things." He thinks about his eyes. In earlier stanzas he committed himself to looking at God's way and to God's path. Yet now he acknowledges the temptation to turn his eyes from God's ways toward worthless things. Both inward and outward temptations press upon him even as he seeks to walk obediently before the Lord. 1 John 2:14-15 might come to mind. The apostle warns us about the lust of the flesh, the lust of the eyes, and the pride of life—the love of the world and the things that are in it. Our psalmist is determined to live obediently to God and his law yet feels the weight of the dangers John identified.

What a good reminder this is for us. Times of trouble and trial often alert us to our worldliness that is easy to miss when life is good. Our spiritual senses wake up when things we take for granted day-by-day are cast into doubt suddenly. The loss of our health, our job, our business, our investments, our relationships—whatever it might be—compels us to consider what is valuable to us. Upon what do we set our eyes? Where are our desires? The psalmist, in his time of trial, deprived of the things that he took for granted, recognized the spiritual realities underlying his suffering. It is a good reminder. We should take spiritual stock during periods of trial. We must grapple with what is valuable and with what is worthless.

Yet even as the psalmist recognizes and expresses this uneasiness, the last three verses of this fifth stanza take quite an interesting turn. In the earlier verses, all his petitions focused upon himself. They asked God to do a kind of internal work in him. He wanted God to teach him, to give him understanding, to incline his heart, and to turn his eyes. But in these final verses, the psalmist shifts his focus. Now he asks the Lord to do a work outside of him, as it were. It is as if he realizes that his own heart and his own obedience are not going to be enough to deliver him from his troubles. Amid the sojourning, persecution, and affliction of this life, he wants God to do a great work for him in this world.

He says in verse 38: "Confirm to your servant your promise." Verse 39 adds: "Turn away the reproach that I dread"—as if he wants God to act against those who oppose him. Then in verse 40 he writes: "Behold, I long for your precepts; in your righteousness give me life." This last phrase may be worth special attention. We should read it alongside the end of verse 39, which is better translated as "for your judgments are good." Against this background the psalmist writes: "in your righteousness give me life." Since we are sinners, it is not immediately clear that God's righteousness and judgments should instill us with confidence. Reflecting on God's righteousness and judgments reminds us that God is just in all his ways. He pays back evil to the wicked—sooner or later. How can the psalmist find confidence in God's righteousness and judgments in light of the justice of God against sin?

The psalmist does not say. He does not say anywhere in Psalm 119, in fact. But the psalmist knew that God had made promises to Abraham, Isaac, and Jacob. God had promised that he would never abandon his people. He could not break those commitments. Despite their sin, he would not forsake them. God's own righteousness was implicated. God would not leave his people in their affliction forever. In his righteousness he would act. He would offer judgments to vindicate his people. Our psalmist did not know exactly how God was going to fulfill those great promises in his righteousness. But he was confident that he would.

And how thankful we can be that we who live in these last days, under the new covenant, know how God has answered. Consider Romans 3. After Paul finished laying out God's indictment against the sin of the entire human race and the just judgments that sin deserved, Paul wrote in Romans 3:21 that the *righteousness* of God has been revealed, apart from the law, through faith in Jesus Christ. God showed his righteousness and that commitment to his people that he could not violate. He showed it by sending his Son. And Jesus Christ showed forth the righteousness of God in his perfect obedience, as Paul explained in Romans 5. The righteousness of Christ has become the great center of our confidence before God. As Paul said a couple of times in Romans 5, we have the righteousness of life through the obedience of Christ. Our psalmist cried out: "In your righteousness give me life." Though he could not describe God's answer to that plea, Paul has done so for us.

Thank God that amid affliction and trial we know that God's judgment on behalf of his people is just and right, as well as merciful and gracious. He has fulfilled his promises in the righteousness of our Lord Jesus Christ.

* * * * *

The sixth stanza begins in verse 41 on much the same note. As the psalmist ended the fifth stanza by appealing to God's righteousness, so in verse 41 he appeals to God's "steadfast love" and his "salvation." These are great themes the Scriptures often use to represent God's action on behalf of his people.

In the next verses, beginning with verse 42, he says: "Then shall I have an answer for him who taunts me, for I trust in your word." How proper that the psalmist, after reflecting on the righteousness, steadfast love, and salvation of God, turns to this idea of trust. This is exactly what God's people do. When we recognize our affliction and weakness and know that God must act for us, we look to him in faith. We look outside of ourselves and trust in him. In fact, think again of those verses we considered earlier in Romans 3. Romans 3:21-22 explains that the righteousness of God has been revealed, through faith in Jesus Christ. When God reveals his righteousness, faith is the proper response. And the psalmist also indicates that faith expresses itself verbally. He writes in verse 42, "Then shall I have an answer for him who taunts me," and he adds in verse 43: "Take not the word of truth utterly out of my mouth." Here and elsewhere in Scripture, God's people confess with their lips what they believe in their hearts. Paul spoke about this later in Romans, in 10:9: "If you confess with your mouth that Jesus is Lord and believe in your heart that God raised him from the dead, you will be saved." Our psalmist combines faith and confession in a similar way.

In verse 42, he reflects on the fact that he has an answer for him who taunts him. Before whom do we make our confession of our faith? While we make it before God, to be sure, we also make it before each other. Lord's Day after Lord's Day, one of the things we do in our worship is confess our faith before God and our fellow saints. We cannot do this when we are unable to meet together in person. In this text, however, the psalmist focuses on the confession we make, not before fellow believers, but before the world. We confess the name of God even before those who ridicule us. We take his name upon our tongues before the world.

Then, in verse 43, the psalmist asks for this word of truth not to be taken out of his mouth because "my hope is in your rules"—or better, "in your judgments." How fitting that he turns to hope, for hope springs from faith. And Scripture makes clear that we have a *sure* hope. The hope that grows out of faith is not uncertain. This sort of hope is not a mere desire for things we want. The world "hopes" for a lot of things, but it has no idea if it will receive them. But when we believers hope in the Lord, based on the promises of his word, we can be certain. We can be sure God's judgments are for us. He has acted for us in the past and he will act again on our behalf. Of that we may be confident.

It is understandable, then, that as the stanza continues through verses 44, 45, and 46, the psalmist breaks out into a new kind of confidence before the Lord. As noted earlier, in the previous stanza there was nothing but petition, verse after verse. Every single verse was a prayer asking the Lord to do something. But in this Waw stanza the number of petitions drops precipitously. Now the psalmist seems to brim with confidence after he has cried out to God and believed that he would answer him in his righteousness and steadfast love. We see it first in verse 44: "I will keep your law continually, forever and ever." He has confidence in God's work of sanctification: the Lord will enable him to believe and to keep his law. Then in verse 45 he says: "I shall walk in a wide place." He suggests that the Lord will rescue him from these afflictions and enemies who stand in his way. God will give him plenty of room to walk. Then he says in verse 46: "I will...speak of your testimonies before kings and shall not be put to shame." Earlier in the psalm, the psalmist expressed fear of being put to shame. He also spoke about princes who were plotting against him. Yet here the psalmist, with renewed confidence, says that he will speak God's testimonies before kings. It is as if the tables turned. No longer do these rulers speak against him, but now he speaks to these rulers and testifies of God's wonderful works to them.

So, we are heartened to see the psalmist expressing this newfound confidence. But as we approach the end of this sixth stanza, the psalmist continues to remind us that he has not attained these blessings yet. He remains confident of God's answer to his prayers, and yet he cannot describe exactly how God is going to answer. The psalmist has not experienced it yet. Has he really been given the opportunity to testify before kings? Has God relieved him of persecution from those who stand against him? The very next stanza indicates not, for the psalmist again reflects on his afflictions and on the insolent people that deride him. No, the psalmist has not received all these answers yet, although he knows that somehow God will answer.

What the psalmist can do is turn back once again to what he does know. And what he does know is the law, the word of the old covenant. In these last two verses, 47-48, he finds delight again in the commandments, which he loves. He lifts his hands toward God's commandments. He mediates on his statutes. He turns back to the law.

Again, how thankful we can be that we have seen the answer of God so much more fully than this psalmist, who could only look forward in confidence and eager anticipation. The last verse of this stanza says: "I will lift up my hands toward your commandments." This reminds us of Paul's words from 1 Timothy 2:8, in the New Testament: "I desire then that in every place the men should pray, lifting holy hands without anger or quarreling." In Scripture, the idea of lifting hands before the Lord can be very literal. When we are looking to God in times of affliction, sometimes the most natural thing to do is to raise our hands to him. But it can also be a metaphorical way to speak about prayer. Whether physically or not, we lift our hands to God when we pray. God's people have always done this. Our psalmist lifted his hands to God's law, which is a way of saying that he lifted them up to God himself, the one who gave his word to his people.

* * * * *

But Paul describes lifting holy hands to God in a much more marvelous way. In 1 Timothy 2:8 Paul said that he wants men to lift holy hands *in every place*. Think back now to the psalmist's condition. He was a sojourner, cast away from his home. That was a curse. To be exiled from the holy land was a sign of God's judgment under the Mosaic law. Israelite exiles were not just banished from the holy land but also from the temple. During the exile, the temple was destroyed. That was the place of prayer. That was the place where God especially wished his people to lift holy hands. Today, we Christians too are a scattered people. We are scattered every Lord's Day insofar as we meet not at a single temple but in many locations throughout the world. We indeed meet "in every place." And that is *not* a curse. In the Great Commission, Christ declared his will that the gospel should go to all nations so that he would have disciples everywhere. What a blessing that the Lord's word has gone throughout the world, and wherever Christians meet they may lift holy hands to God in prayer.

And this is a comfort for us in times of pandemic and lockdown. What we did in 2020—tuning in online—is not the way we want to call upon God. We don't do it that way when we don't have to. In those days not only were churches scattered throughout the world but also members of the same congregation were separated from each other as they were confined to their own homes. Yet praise God that even under such circumstances we may lift holy hands to God in prayer—in every place, in every home, and in every room.

And we know that he hears us! We can have even greater confidence than the psalmist of old. We learn why if we back up a few verses in 1 Timothy 2. Paul spoke about lifting holy hands in every place shortly after saying that there's "one God, and… one mediator between God and men, the man Christ Jesus, who gave himself as a ransom for all, which is the testimony given at the proper time." God had not yet given that testimony during the psalmist's days. But now he has. Jesus Christ is the mediator, the one mediator between God and man. And as the Epistle to the Hebrews describes so wonderfully, that mediator has finished his work of redemption, he has gone through the heavens, he is seated at the right hand of God and has opened up a new and living way. Thus our worship, every Lord's Day, joins in the worship taking place in the heavenly sanctuary. Wherever we meet on earth, our true meeting location is in heaven. Christ, the one great, final high priest, is in that new-creation temple. Because of him we can worship in every place—not in an earthly temple, but wherever we find ourselves.

Please also note that Paul, in 1 Timothy 2, spoke of lifting holy hands in every place just after stating that God desires all people to be saved and to come to a knowledge of the truth. Salvation is not just for Israelites in a particular holy land, worshiping at a holy temple on earth. God desires all people to be saved. In every place, among every kind of people, God sends out his gospel and desires that all hear and be saved. And at the beginning of 1 Timothy 2 Paul wrote: "I urge that supplications, prayers, intercessions, and thanksgivings be made for all people, for kings and all who are in high positions." As we lift holy hands in prayer, we pray for all sorts of people, even for our civil authorities. What a timely reminder for us. Every day the news bombards us with evidence about how weak, ignorant, and helpless our civil authorities are. We and others are tempted to despise and condemn our civil authorities. Or maybe you are putting your hope in our civil authorities to solve our crisis. Whatever your political opinions at present, Paul exhorts us here to pray for our civil authorities. He says we should do this so we might live peaceful and quiet lives. But since God desires all to be saved, that must include our civil authorities. They are weak and ignorant—which is only to say that they need God's grace, as the rest of us.

As we come to the end of this part of Psalm 119, and also of these beautiful verses in 1 Timothy 2, let us be people of prayer, even during uneasy times. Like the psalmist, may we lift petition after petition to our Lord. And may we believe his promises by faith, knowing that in his righteousness and steadfast love he has acted for his people and will never leave us or forsake us. Lift holy hands in prayer, in the name of our mediator Jesus Christ, in every place and for all people. Praise God that we have such a mediator in times of trouble.

4

Remembering in the Night

Psalm 119:49-64

If one thing comes to mind when you think about Psalm 119, it is that this is a very long reflection upon the word of God. It uses many different terms for God's word, repeated throughout these many verses. But another thing Psalm 119 does is offer a window into the spiritual experience of an old covenant saint. We cannot be certain who the author of the psalm is. He does not give his name. But we know he was a godly, thoughtful, and eloquent person. The Holy Spirit also inspired him. As we read the psalm, we get insight into his spiritual experience. He opens his heart for us as he describes his wrestling before God.

We also learn that this psalmist was a sojourner. Most old covenant saints could not have said this, at least not in the way our psalmist meant. Israel lived under the Mosaic law in the Promised Land of Israel. They were supposed to be a settled people, not sojourners. The people possessed the land. Different tribes and families owned their own plots of ground. That was their inheritance from God, to be passed down from one generation to the next. Yet our psalmist was a sojourner, apparently away from his family land. He was most likely away from the Promised Land altogether, living as a foreigner among pagan Gentiles. And life was not easy for him. It was full of affliction, trouble, struggles, and persecution.

This is so helpful for us to consider because the New Testament tells us that we are sojourners—for example, in 1 Peter 2. Every single new covenant believer is a sojourner. This is not because you are not settled in an earthly home. You may have lived in your earthly home for a long time. We are all sojourners because our true home is the new creation. Our citizenship is in heaven. Every single one of us is a sojourner, no matter how recently we changed earthly addresses.

To be sure, our experience as sojourners is not identical to that of the author of Psalm 119. We need to pay attention to those differences as well. But in important respects we should sympathize with his experience as a sojourner and seek to learn from it. And one of the things to learn, which emerges in these two stanzas we are considering now, is that amid the trials and struggles that sojourners have while away from home, we ought to *remember*. Remembering should comfort and encourage us. We remember the word of God and the past work of God on our behalf. As we do, God also draws us to look forward to what he is going to accomplish: the full and final deliverance of his people.

* * * * *

We look first at verses 49-56, the Zayin stanza. At this point Psalm 119 changes its tone or mood. In the previous two stanzas—beginning at the end of He and then throughout Waw—the psalmist hit a high note. He expressed a great deal of joy and confidence. He wrote about the righteousness, steadfast love, and salvation of God. He obviously felt encouraged. He experienced this confidence as he walked before God, even as he faced the enemies around him. Yet we come now to the Zayin stanza and suddenly the psalmist is back to reflecting on his troubles and suffering. Notice how he puts it in verse 51: "The insolent utterly deride me." The insolent—that is, the arrogant or boastful—are not only dragging him down but doing it *utterly*, to an extreme measure.

As we reflect on this change of tone, it is worth thinking for a moment about the ups and downs of Psalm 119. Those of you who have tried to read Psalm 119 know it can be a difficult endeavor. One thing that makes it challenging is the feeling that the psalm is not really going anywhere. When you read narratives in Scripture it is easy to see how you move from point A to point B. If you read one of Paul's Epistles you can follow the logic of his argument. But none of this is true when you read Psalm 119. You get to the end, and it may seem that you are in the same place where you started. Now, there is a sense in which that is true. You are not just imagining that. The psalmist repeatedly circles back to many of the same themes. But that is not an accident. It is certainly not because the psalmist lacks artistic ability as a poet. One reason the psalmist constructs his poem in the way he does, I suggest, is to mirror the spiritual life of a sojourner. You are a Christian sojourner. Do you ever feel as though you are not making much progress in your spiritual life? Do you ever feel that sins you struggled with years ago come back again to trouble you? Christians have times of joy and of confidence before the Lord but then confront again periods of struggle, melancholy, and sorrow. That is life in this world for new covenant Christians. And it was life for this psalmist as a sojourner.

There is real movement in Psalm 119. It does not always work in a straight line. The movement of Psalm 119 is back and forth and up and down. It reflects our own spiritual experience in this world, so perhaps that can be encouraging to us as we study Psalm 119.

We can see a change of mood or tone in another way as well. As the psalmist reflects upon his hardship and persecution here, he responds differently from what we saw earlier in the psalm. Earlier, the psalmist's main response to affliction was to pray. In a sense, Psalm 119 is one long prayer. But within Psalm 119, some of the verses themselves are prayers, in that they make requests or petitions to God. Yet many verses are not prayers but only statements. In the opening five stanzas the psalmist used an increasing number of prayers. The psalmist was feeling increasingly afflicted and kept calling out more to God for help. That is indeed one thing we believers do amid trouble. When we feel afflicted, we pray. But note what the psalmist does here in verse 49, the first verse of this stanza. He does make one petition—"Remember your word"—but that is the only one. It is the only prayer in this entire stanza. It is interesting that this pattern continues in the next stanza, which we consider next. It too has few petitions.

What the psalmist does here instead is reflect. Another way to put it is that he is meditating. This is another thing godly people do when they face affliction. We do not only pray, important as that is. We reflect. We take stock. We meditate before the Lord. One way to describe meditation is reflecting in the presence of God. This is what the psalmist primarily does in this stanza. And a crucial part of meditation is remembering. For some reason I do not understand, the ESV uses the verb "think" in verse 52 where "remember" is the preferable translation. So, in verse 52, the psalmist says: "when I remember your rules from of old." And then again in verse 55: "I remember your name in the night, O LORD." Thus, the psalmist says, "I remember" twice in this stanza. Yet perhaps you noticed that the stanza mentions remembering even before these two references. The very first word of the stanza is "Remember." Before the psalmist *himself* remembers before God in his meditation, he asked *God* to remember: "Remember your word to your servant."

How proper that is. We need God to remember his words to us. God has made promises to us. God has pledged to be our God and to help us. Of course, we know that God will not forget. He cannot forget. He knows all things at every moment. But as we turn to God amid our trouble, we have the liberty to approach him and say: "Lord, please do not forget. Remember all that you have promised us." We can be encouraged as we pray, since we know that God will do exactly what we ask. And because of this confidence in God, we ourselves can remember in turn. We can ponder what God has promised in the past and be assured that he will be faithful to all of it.

God will show the same grace and mercy to his people in the future that he has shown them in the past. As the psalmist puts it in verse 49, he has *hope* because of the word that God remembers. In verses 50 and 52 he adds that he has comfort.

Later in this service we will celebrate the Lord's Supper. One of the wonderful things about the Lord's Supper is that it calls us to remember: "Do this in remembrance of me." The psalmist could think back to the exodus from Egypt or the promises to Abraham and know that God was on his side. But we have the even greater privilege to remember that God gave his Son, who offered himself up for us. If God did this for us in the past, he will help us now and in the future. He still gives us comfort and hope amid our afflictions.

We turn now to the second part of this Zayin stanza, beginning in verse 53. Suddenly, the psalmist changes his mood again. He makes a striking statement in verse 53: "Hot indignation seizes me because of the wicked, who forsake your law." That is a way of saying that he became truly angry, but the way he put it was intentional. He does not say, "I got angry."

Rather, he suggests that anger itself acted on him. This anger was like an outside power that suddenly took control of him. That is indeed our experience when we get angry or have other strong emotions. We feel as though it is not really us. It is as if some outside force has gripped us. That can be disturbing. Our emotions seem out of our control. But if we honestly reflect and meditate, as believers should do, the way we experience emotions provides insight into ourselves. What makes you really angry? Or what makes you really sad, happy, or anxious? The answers to such questions reveal what is in our hearts and show what is really important to us. When you feel as though anger seizes you, is it because of something important? Is it something worth getting angry about, or is it something trivial or petty? Notice why indignation seized the psalmist: because of wicked people who forsake the law of God. That is something worthy of anger. This reveals our psalmist's noble heart.

Yet how quickly things turn again. The psalmist makes one brief, impassioned statement about his anger and then in the next verses, 54-55, he writes: "Your statutes have been my songs in the house of my sojourning. I remember your name in the night, O LORD." The psalmist is seized by anger at one moment and is singing songs to God the next. You might inquire about yourself. When you get really, really angry, how often do you feel like bursting into song and praying to the Lord? These things do not usually go together. But our psalmist does not remain angry for long. As Paul wonderfully said in Ephesians 4:26: "be angry and do not sin; do not let the sun go down on your anger." Our psalmist was seized by anger. Yet, after sundown, in the middle of the night, he sings songs to the Lord. He was not overcome by anger but turns to worship as he continues his meditations before God.

It is important to note here that the psalmist's troubles have not gone away. He says he is in the house of *sojourning*. This is an ominous reference. He reminds himself and his readers that he is away from the Promised Land of blessing. He is away from the people of God. Verse 55 adds to this ominous tone by telling us *when* he sings and remembers: in the night. Night usually has negative connotations in Scripture. Morning is the time of joy and deliverance, while night is the time of uneasiness, danger, and fear. The psalmist is in the midst of night. In a way, this is what it means to be a sojourner. Sojourners feel as though it is always night, metaphorically. Our psalmist did not happen to get up in the middle of the night and share his thoughts. Sojourners are creatures of the night, spiritually, because night stands for fear and trouble.

But the psalmist's response is remarkable. He cries out to God, remembers his name, and sings before him. The stanza ends in verse 56. I am going to suggest a modified translation. The ESV has: "This blessing has fallen to me." The word "blessing" is not there in the original Hebrew, which simply says: "this has fallen to me" or "this is the way it is for me." Translations thus struggle to know exactly how to fill that in. What exactly has fallen to him? The psalmist may simply be looking back at what he has been talking about and saying: "This is how it is for me." I suggest the translation: "This is how it is for me that I have kept your precepts." This is indeed how things are for those of us who want to obey God's law and yet live in the night, in the house of sojourning. The evil in this world makes us angry. We experience affliction. We are persecuted. And yet we remember our God and turn to him in song, even amid the night.

* * * * *

We now move to the next stanza, Heth. And what a wonderful way it begins: "The Lord is my portion." I call it wonderful because it is such a great reminder here in Psalm 119.

Psalm 119, on the whole, is one grand meditation on the law of God, or on the word of God generally. Yet we are reminded here that God's word is not the most important thing, as important as it is. God himself is most important. God's word is only great because it points us to God. God's word is only a blessing because it brings us into blessed fellowship with him. The Lord, he says, is my portion. That is an amazing idea. To say that God is your portion is to say, "I have a share in God. God belongs to me." The Old Testament says several times that we, his people, are God's portion. We are his inheritance. Yet the psalmist can also say that God is *our* portion. Elsewhere Scripture says that God is our inheritance. As we enter into covenant with God, by his grace, it goes both ways. He claims us for himself, and we claim him as our own.

We find something similar in the next verse, 58: "I entreat your favor with all my heart." Literally, the Hebrew says: "I seek your face with my heart." We do not seek God's favor independently from seeking God. We seek the face of God himself. This is a way to express intimacy with him. He is our portion, and thus we may approach his very face. That is where God's word points us. God's word never stands alone. It directs us to God in faith and worship.

Yet there's also spiritual tension in these opening two verses of the stanza, although perhaps not readily evident. Put yourself again in the shoes of this psalmist. He has told us a couple of times now that he is a sojourner, which indicates that he is away from the Promised Land. But the Promised Land was where God appointed old covenant believers under Moses to experience him as their portion and inheritance. In fact, the Old Testament sometimes spoke of the Promised Land itself as their portion and inheritance. The land was where they could gather and worship, offer their sacrifices, and receive the blessing and forgiveness of God. But as a sojourner away from that land, our psalmist was distant from his earthly portion and inheritance. So verses 57 and 58 are a remarkable statement of faith. It is as if he says: "Lord, although I'm away from your Promised Land and your temple, although I am in the midst of enemies, I believe that you are still my portion, even if I cannot see it with my eyes." He believes that God is still his God and that he can still seek his face. The psalmist expresses great faith, but he must have been very puzzled as to how God would resolve it all.

As we consider verses 59-62, we again see movement. But here it is the movement of the psalmist's eyes. His focus moves. As noted earlier, in the first two verses of the stanza the psalmist continued his meditation by focusing on God himself. God was his portion and he sought his face. But now he says: "When I think on my ways...." This is part of godly meditation. Our meditations reflect on God, his word, his promises, and his deeds. But our meditations should turn back to ourselves as well. Who are we before God? How are we walking before him? As the psalmist ponders his own ways, he tells us what he sees. In verse 59: "I turn my feet to your testimonies." In verse 60: "I hasten and do not delay to keep your commandments." He resolves once again to walk in God's ways—and not slowly or lethargically. Rather, he *hastens* to go in that path that God has set before him.

Then, in verses 61-62, we see a recap of something in the previous stanza. The psalmist reminds us that he is suffering. In verse 61 he reflects on the cords of the wicked that ensnare him. Then in verse 62 he speaks again of the *night*. At midnight, he rises before God. Night symbolizes a time of suffering, but, as verse 61 also notes, our psalmist does not forget God's law. To put that positively: he remembers. Thus he returns to the theme of remembering God. When he arises in the middle of the night, during the fear and the anxiety that nighttime represents, his mind returns to God and his word.

And with that, we come to the final two verses of our text. Although much in this stanza looks similar to the Zayin stanza, the psalmist brings out a couple of new ideas worth considering briefly.

In verse 63 the psalmist mentions something he has not noted yet. Up to this point, the psalmist speaks as though he is all by himself. In the opening verses he did say: "Blessed are *those* whose way is blameless…. Blessed are *those* who keep his testimonies." But except for that, he gives the impression of being alone. He has used "I," "me," and "my." But here in verse 63 he writes: "I am a companion of all who fear you, of those who keep your precepts." In a way, it is not surprising that the psalmist has felt alone and that his psalm seems individualistic. That is often the fate of a sojourner. For the psalmist, being away from the holy land entailed being away from the holy people. He was unable to worship at the temple with the throngs of God's worshippers. As a sojourner in exile, he probably did feel lonely.

Even so, the psalmist writes: "I am a companion of all who fear you." He seems to say something like this: "I cannot see the congregation of your people. I may not be one of the throngs going up to Jerusalem to worship. But I know that I have a bond of fellowship with all those who call upon your name." This is another great expression of faith. God has never intended his people to be solitary believers. He has ordained that all who have communion with him also have communion with one another—even with fellow believers we cannot see. The psalmist professes faith that he has companions, even during his loneliness.

And then in the final verse he states: "The earth, O LORD, is full of your steadfast love; teach me your statutes." There seems to be some ambiguity here. Ambiguity is when you say something that could be interpreted in more than one way. The Hebrew word for "earth" could also simply mean "land." It is possible that the psalmist means: "The land, O Lord—the Promised Land—is full of your steadfast love." But the ESV is correct to translate this as "earth." The psalmist is a sojourner away from the land. We know that he seeks hope and comfort in his "house of sojourning," as he put it earlier. And during that, he can say, "O Lord, the earth is full of your steadfast love." The whole earth is full of God's steadfast love—not just Jerusalem or Canaan. The Lord loves his whole creation. This means that he loves more than Israelites. That may have been difficult for the psalmist to say, because in those days the Jerusalem temple was *the* place for the worship of God. Yet the Old Testament itself made great promises about a coming day when God's word would spread far abroad. Isaiah, for example, said God would raise up a Servant of the Lord to be a light to the ends of the earth and to be a covenant for the nations. Our psalmist, during his affliction, found hope and encouragement in the prospect of this coming great work of God, however difficult it must have been for him to envision exactly how God would do it.

* * * * *

Therefore, be encouraged as new covenant sojourners. We do not have a holy land here and now. We do not have a permanent home on this earth. Christians must live amid suffering and persecution. We endure what sometimes is a long night. But as the psalmist remembered God's great deeds of old to Israel, so we can remember even greater things: the life, death, and resurrection of Christ on our behalf. The God who raised him from the dead is on your side. As Paul said in Romans 5, if this God has given his own Son for you, even while you were enemies, how much more will he rescue you from the wrath to come? What will he not give you if he has done *that* for you?

The psalmist also looked ahead to God's grace to the ends of the earth. But what was future for the psalmist is something we can remember today, and indeed it is still ongoing. God has sent his gospel to the ends of the earth and continues to call people from all tribes, nations, and languages. We are living proof of that at this very moment. God has kept his word.

And as we endure our sojourn here, we have companions. God has established a church that he wills to exist in every corner of the globe. In 1 Peter 2, where Peter said that Christians are sojourners and exiles, he also wrote: "You are a chosen race, a royal priesthood, a holy nation." The promises God gave to Israel of old are now yours as the church of Jesus Christ. Do not think lightly of the companions the Lord has given you! He has given you brothers and sisters in the faith. Pandemics and other things provide excuses to neglect Christian fellowship and corporate worship. But do not forsake the body of Christ! Companions along our sojourning way are among God's greatest gifts. So let us remember our God and give him thanks, both as individuals and together.

5

Affliction, Repentance, and Restoration

Psalm 119:65-80

There are many things the author of the Long Psalm does not tell us about himself and his situation. We would like to know a lot more! But the Lord has told us exactly what we need to know about the psalmist in order to read Psalm 119 profitably. Among the things we do know is that he had experienced and continued to experience times of great trouble. We know that he struggled with his own sin. We know that he faced persecution. On many occasions he complained about the evil people who afflicted him, even seeking his life on account of his faith.

The psalmist also tells us that he is a sojourner on the earth, and this too is helpful for interpreting and profiting from his psalm. The psalmist was not at home and did not enjoy peace and prosperity in the Promised Land that God gave to Israel long before. Perhaps he was one of the exiles in Babylon. By telling us that he is a sojourner, the psalmist signals that things have gone terribly wrong with him and with the people of

God. Being expelled from the Promised Land and driven into foreign lands was one of the prime curses God had threatened to bring against his people if they rebelled against him.

This context is an important reason why Psalm 119 has spoken so powerfully to so many Christians through the years, for the New Testament tells us that we too are sojourners in this world—not sojourners because we have been expelled from an earthly promised land but because we are not in heaven yet. We are citizens of heaven. We have an everlasting inheritance in God's new creation in Christ. Yet we are called to live here, among many enemies of the faith, enduring many trials that test our perseverance and sometimes lead us to question our Lord himself.

The two stanzas in Psalm 119 we now consider—in verses 65-80—open a window into the psalmist's spiritual experience. He reflects on God's purposes in bringing him through these trials. What is their point? Why would God allow one of his servants to suffer as he does? What is the result of all this? I suggest that these stanzas are among the most crucial in Psalm 119. They answer a question that has been building for several stanzas about why a righteous man, such as our psalmist, suffers so severely. The psalmist reveals some information about his past. He also concludes that God was good and faithful in bringing him through these trials. But that is not all. These trials were not only good for him but also good for his fellow believers who saw God's grace and faithfulness to him during such hardships. We as well should contemplate God's grace and faithfulness to our psalmist and find great encouragement in our own trials.

* * * * *

We look first at verses 65-72, the Teth stanza. The twenty-two stanzas of Psalm 119 are organized according to the letters of the Hebrew alphabet. In our stanza, each verse in the original Hebrew begins with the letter Teth. A common Hebrew word that begins with this letter is a term for "good." The psalmist takes advantage of this: five of these eight stanzas begin with this Hebrew word. The psalmist thus signals that goodness is a major theme of the stanza. I should mention, incidentally, that this does not mean that in each of these five verses you will see the word "good" in your English Bibles. For example, in the first verse, 65, the ESV reads: "You have dealt well with your servant." In this case, "well" translates that Hebrew word for "good." An alternative translation, to bring out the point I am making, might be: "You have done what is *good* for your servant." As we consider this stanza, therefore, keep in mind this theme of goodness.

So the psalmist begins by writing that God has done what is good for his servant, according to his word. As we might expect, this stanza speaks first of goodness with respect to God. God is good and he does what is good for his people. In verse 66, the psalmist requests something for himself: "Teach me good judgment and knowledge." God's people wish to reflect God's goodness. The theme of goodness continues in verse 68, where the psalmist uses the word twice, again with respect to God and his work: "You are good and do good; teach me your statutes." Hence, the psalmist sets goodness before us from the outset of the stanza.

But also note what he says in verse 67, the third verse, amid these statements about God's goodness: "Before I was afflicted, I went astray, but now I keep your word." Think about this for a moment. The psalmist is reflecting on the goodness of God. But when a person is focused on God's goodness, he is probably *not* inclined to think about his suffering. Yet, this is exactly what the psalmist brings to our attention. In the midst of reflecting on God's goodness, he also reflects on his own affliction. And this is a good exercise for us as we follow the psalmist's lead. He makes us do something we are not comfortable doing.

Consider what exactly the psalmist says. He confesses that before he was afflicted he went astray, but now he keeps God's word. With this, we begin to get a sense of why his suffering came to mind while he was thinking about God's goodness. This psalmist was a rebel against God. He did not mention this previously in the psalm. The way he speaks in this verse indicates that he had suffered a particular affliction. Amidst his many sufferings, he must have experienced one particular, extreme hardship. Before that affliction, he was a rebel. But he endured that affliction, and now he keeps God's word. That affliction brought him to repentance. He must have reconsidered his ways. He took his sufferings to heart. He turned back to God. He does not say this directly, but it seems that the extreme affliction he endured was becoming a sojourner. Because he strayed from God's word, God sent him into exile. It was a terrible blow. But now he has seen God's goodness in this affliction because it was instrumental in turning him away from his rebellion against God. It resulted in his moral reformation.

The psalmist will come back to this theme in a moment. But first he takes two verses—69 and 70—to reflect upon the evil people he talks about so often in Psalm 119. The psalmist does not mention goodness in these two verses. He talks about goodness through all the rest of the stanza, but when he speaks about evildoers the word "good" disappears. Evildoers are the opposite of good. These wicked people who wish him harm confront him repeatedly. They are not good people. He says some colorful things about them. They not only "smear" him with lies but their heart is also "unfeeling like fat." That is not an expression you have used anytime recently, but it is surely not a compliment! We do speak of some people as tender-hearted.

We know what that means. To have a heart that is unfeeling like fat seems to be the opposite. These people are ever before him, and he will reflect on them again later in our text.

After commenting on these wicked who are the opposite of good, the psalmist returns to the theme of goodness. In verse 71 he says explicitly what he implied earlier in the stanza: "It is good for me that I was afflicted, that I might learn your statutes." His affliction was for his spiritual welfare. It produced a greater understanding of God and his word. Undoubtedly this psalmist knew about God's word previously. But by enduring this affliction he reached a deeper understanding of God. He took his suffering to heart, and now he has perceived the depths of God's word in a new way.

He expresses this in a wonderfully poetic way in verse 72: "The law of your mouth is better to me than thousands of gold and silver pieces." ("Better" is the translation of "good" in this context.) One of the things the psalmist learned by going through this great affliction is that God's word is the most valuable thing in the world. A common human temptation is to think and act as if the things the world values are better than the word of God, and the psalmist fell into that temptation. Think about what he is saying here. The law of God is better than thousands of gold and silver pieces. We can easily understand this sort of imagery. Gold and silver were valuable in the time the psalmist wrote, as they remain today. In fact, gold has a reputation for retaining its value over time. This is why gold prices tend to go up in times of political or financial crisis. There is something stable about gold.

Let us do a little calculation to appreciate the psalmist's point. If gold holds its value over time, then what "thousands of pieces of gold" means to us today is similar to what it meant to the psalmist and his original readers. Think about a thousand pieces of gold today. People often use one-ounce coins to store and distribute gold, so let us assume coins of that size. In that case, a thousand gold pieces at current prices are worth more than two million dollars. And the psalmist speaks of *thousands*—not just one thousand, but multiple thousands of gold and silver pieces. It is as if the psalmist is saying: "Your word, Lord, is more valuable than millions and millions of dollars. The most valuable thing in the world's eyes—your word is far more valuable than that." He learned that through the affliction he had suffered.

Think about this a little further. As I mentioned, this psalmist may well be an exile in Babylon. He may have experienced the horrible event when the Babylonians ransacked Jerusalem and exiled many of God's people to their city in the east. Even if the psalmist lived at an earlier point in Israel's history, his words would have spoken powerfully to those who experienced this later exile. We read about these events in the final chapters of 2 Kings. These are very dark chapters of Scripture. They narrate so much stupid rebellion against the Lord and how the Lord brought well-deserved judgment against his people. It is interesting that gold makes appearances several times in these final chapters of 2 Kings. We can understand why this was on the psalmist's mind if he lived through this experience.

2 Kings 23 tells about Jehoiakim, the third-to-last king of Judah. Pharaoh, king of Egypt, came against him and forced him to give up the gold and silver he had stored. Then in the next chapter, 2 Kings 24, we read about the second-to-last king of Judah, Jehoiachin. In this account, the Babylonians came against him, sent him into exile, and took gold and silver from the temple. Finally, 2 Kings 25 describes the last king of Judah, Zedekiah. The Babylonians finished their destruction of Jerusalem and again took gold and silver from the temple, whatever may have remained.

It is clear what was going on. These kings of Judah were storing up their worldly treasures! They must have thought it was going to be a bulwark for them. Surely they would be safe if they stored up enough gold! Meanwhile, they forsook the word of God, rebelling against their Lord. And what happened? A lot of good that gold did them. Pharaoh took some of it away. Nebuchadnezzar took the rest of it. The psalmist may have been eyewitness of these events, or at least foresaw them— and he learned. He learned that God's word is so much more valuable. It is so much more powerful than the gold, silver, and all the treasures of this world. Our wealth will do nothing for us in the end if we forsake God and his word.

This judgment which came upon Jerusalem was horrible. It was a sign and foretaste of the final judgment. Yet it was not the final judgment. God was not done with his people, as rebellious as they were. And this gave opportunity for God's people at that time to take these things to heart, to repent of their sins, and to turn again to God in his word. This is what our psalmist did. God had promised long ago in the law of Moses that even after Israel had disobeyed and he had exiled them, he would renew his grace to his people. And the psalmist experienced this too. He took his suffering to heart and turned back to God. This should also be an encouragement to us. That becomes clear in our next stanza.

* * * * *

In the Yodh stanza, the psalmist broadens his scope. This is not only about him, but about all the people of God as well.

This stanza begins in verse 73 with a confession of faith, of sorts. Many times in Psalm 119 the psalmist pauses for a moment and confesses who God is. Here he acknowledges that God is his creator, and he asks for understanding from the one who made him.

But the next verses show that the psalmist has not changed his subject matter. He is still thinking about his sufferings and God's purposes in them. This is clear in verse 75: "I know, O LORD, that your rules are righteous, and that in faithfulness you have afflicted me." In the previous stanza, the psalmist recognized that it was good for him to be afflicted. God was good to him in carrying him through these sufferings because it brought him to repentance. Now he says that God was faithful in afflicting him—a similar way of saying the same thing. But notice the new theme the psalmist brings to our attention, in verse 74, the second verse of the stanza: "Those who fear you shall see me and rejoice, because I have hoped in your word." The psalmist will not be the only one to learn from his afflictions. His fellow believers, who fear the Lord, will look at him and rejoice. They will see his repentance and observe how God was gracious to him, and they will be encouraged. The psalmist's sufferings will strengthen the people of God.

This sort of thing happens in our ordinary experience. We see fellow Christians called to walk through terrible ordeals and we marvel at how they stay faithful as God sustains them. The godly response of others to suffering can be an encouragement to us. But the psalmist does not seem to be talking about ordinary experience. Sometimes God does especially amazing things in calling his servants through suffering for the sake of the people of God in general. The end of 2 Kings, which we considered above, provides a powerful example of this. 2 Kings is very discouraging in many ways since it is full of human rebellion and divine judgment. But the very end of 2 Kings relates that King Jehoiachin, the second-to-last king of Judah, was exiled to Babylon and imprisoned for thirty-seven years. Thirty-seven years in prison was undoubtedly an unpleasant experience. I imagine it was extra unpleasant for a foreign king accused of rebellion against Babylon. But after thirty-seven years, the king of Babylon released Jehoiachin and gave him a place at his own royal table, so that he ate with some honor and dignity for the rest of his life.

Why did 2 Kings end on that note? It was there for the encouragement of the people of God. When God drove Judah into exile and they became sojourners in a foreign land, they must have wondered about the goodness and faithfulness of God, the very things our psalmist reflects on in the stanzas before us. God had promised that a son of David would sit upon the throne of his people forever. Yet there was Jehoiachin, the heir of David's throne, sitting for decades in a Babylonian prison. Had God forgotten his promises? Had his goodness and faithfulness failed? By including that little story at the end of his book, the author of 2 Kings announced that God had not forgotten his promises. Yes, God's people would suffer affliction for their sins, but God was faithful. He would restore the line of David. He would establish a new king to rule his people in righteousness.

That restoration of Jehoiachin pointed to a much greater restoration. Thus if Jehoiachin's restoration after thirty-seven years encouraged the people of God at that time, how much more should that greater future restoration be an encouragement to us? When God restored Jehoiachin and thereby showed his ongoing commitment to the line of David, he was ultimately promising the true son of David, our Lord Jesus Christ, who would rule God's people in righteousness forever and ever. Our Lord Jesus surely knew affliction. Thirty-seven years in a Babylonian prison was bad, but it hardly compares to crucifixion and drinking the cup of God's wrath to its dregs. Jesus knew affliction, and he endured it for your sake. And if the restoration of Jehoiachin after thirty-seven years was great, the resurrection of the Son of God from the dead was infinitely greater. Jesus did not receive a seat at a

Babylonian king's table, but he was seated at the right hand of his Father on high.

Sometimes we doubt God's goodness and faithfulness when we suffer afflictions in this life. We could look to our psalmist or to King Jehoiachin for encouragement. But much better to look to our Lord Jesus Christ. His death and resurrection are proof that suffering is *not* the last word of God for his people. We may suffer affliction for a day, but God will not abandon us. He will never fail to bless us and bring us to glory. We need not doubt that. May we be among the people the psalmist spoke about: "Those who fear you shall see me and rejoice, because I have hoped in your word."

In the next verses, 76-77, the psalmist cries out for God's steadfast love and mercy. He reminds us that he is still suffering. He endured a great affliction, God brought him through and gave him repentance, and that encouraged the people of God. Yet the psalmist is still suffering and so he needs steadfast love and mercy. He notes in verse 78 that insolent people continue to wrong him, and so he asks again that God put them to shame, bringing his judgment upon them. In verse 80, the final verse, he asks that he himself would not be put to shame. The idea of shame connects these two verses, the third-to-last and last verses of the stanza. Our persecuted, sojourning psalmist surely experienced great shame at the time he was writing whereas the wicked people who oppressed him were honored. The persecutors enjoyed respect and glory in this life. Our psalmist says, in effect: "Lord, turn this around! How long will your beloved people be despised in this world?"

What encouragement again the resurrection of our Lord Jesus Christ should be. Our Lord Jesus knew shame as none of us ever will. He hung naked on the cross, exposed to the judgment of man and God. Yet his resurrection radically overturned that shame. He now enjoys all authority in heaven and earth, seated at God's right hand in highest glory. That too is a sign for us. God calls us to take up our cross and follow Christ and hence be exposed to shame in this life for the sake of the gospel. But the day is coming when the Lord will take away our shame forever. He will put his enemies to shame and exalt his people who look to him in faith and hope.

* * * * *

As we come to the end of our text, I want to leave you with verse 79, the second-to-last verse of this stanza: "Let those who fear you turn to me, that they may know your testimonies." What a wonderful thought to close this chapter. This verse revisits an idea in verse 74. There the psalmist stated that those who fear God will see him and rejoice. Here in verse 79 he prays to the Lord, as if saying: "O Lord, make this happen! O Lord, let all those who fear God turn to me, learn your word, and know your testimonies."

So, let us do that. Let us reflect on this psalmist's experience. Let us reflect on his afflictions, his repentance, his deliverance, and now his dedication to the Lord. Let this be an encouragement to us. But do not look only at the psalmist. Do what Hebrews 12 calls us to do: consider Jesus and see what he endured from sinful men. Think about what Jesus endured for you and how God raised him from the dead for your sake.

This provides a great new perspective on our trials. Why do you suffer what you do? Why does God call you to walk through the valley of the shadow of death? Hebrews 12 assures you that it is not because God hates you. It is because God loves you. It is not because God is a wrathful judge who wishes to bring you low and punish you for your sins. No, God is a loving Father, and one of the reasons he allows Christians to suffer is to discipline them for their good, for their correction—to bring forth a harvest of righteousness. How our Father deals with us, his children, is not always pleasant at the time. Hebrews 12 tells us that. But the Lord knows that it is for our good. And we can trust him as a wise and loving Father to bring us through trials that are for our spiritual welfare.

So do not despise the discipline of your heavenly Father. If you despise afflictions from the hand of your heavenly Father, the only alternative is afflictions from the hand of God as an angry judge. Trust in him. He loves you. As he brought his Son through shame on your behalf, so he will bring you through whole, righteous and holy in Christ.

6

Fixed in the Heavens

Psalm 119:81-96

The previous stanzas, Teth and Yodh, emphasized the goodness, righteousness, and faithfulness of God in bringing the psalmist through a great calamity he had suffered—probably referring to his expulsion from the Promised Land and becoming a sojourner, perhaps even an exile in Babylon. The psalmist wrote in these stanzas that he learned from his affliction. He took to heart God's judgment against sin, and he turned back to God. He repented and gained understanding of God's statutes. As he learned from that affliction, he also called his fellow believers to look at him and find encouragement. He invited them to see, through him, that there's hope beyond God's judgment. God's judgment is not the final word for his people. He is a God of mercy for those who look to him.

The psalmist took a big-picture perspective in those previous stanzas. He was able to step back from his present circumstances and consider God's work in his life. Yet his ability to take this big-picture perspective did not change the fact that he was still suffering great trials. The psalmist was still in some sort of exile when he wrote Psalm 119. He had not yet returned home to the Promised Land. God had restored him spiritually in an important sense, and the psalmist had thus tasted of God's goodness, yet he was still suffering.

In the first of the stanzas we now consider, Kaph, the psalmist assesses his present circumstances. He reflects upon his suffering and he paints an exceedingly bleak picture. But his reflections turn suddenly again in Lamed, the second of our stanzas. The shift from Kaph to Lamed is remarkably abrupt. What is especially interesting is that these are the middle stanzas of Psalm 119. It has twenty-two stanzas in total, and these are the eleventh and twelfth. So the middle of our text is exactly the middle of the Long Psalm. What happens at this center point is no accident. The last stanza of the first half is the gloomiest and bleakest of the stanzas while the first stanza of the second half is arguably the most exalted. Here we find the psalmist most amazed at God's greatness, the firmness of his promises, and his grace to his people.

Much of Psalm 119 is sobering and even disheartening. Yet, fundamentally, Psalm 119 is positive and encouraging. For all the psalmist's serious reflection on suffering, he always returns to the sovereign grace of God, lifting his and our spirits. These stanzas remind us that this gracious God is on our side. We belong to him. And because he, his word, and his faithfulness endure, we his people also endure. We stand steadfast in our God.

* * * * *

We look first at the Kaph stanza, verses 81-88, and begin by surveying these verses rapidly. The psalmist voices his distress in various ways, without changing themes much within the stanza. He just finds different expressions, verse by verse, to describe his great suffering.

The psalmist uses the same verb to begin both the first two verses, 81 and 82. The ESV reads: "My soul longs for your salvation…. My eyes long for your promise." That is a valid translation, but this repeated verb needs a little more explanation. To use English idioms, this verb communicates, in context, that the psalmist is at the end of his rope or that his tank is running close to empty. You might think of this as the longing of a traveler in the desert who is about to die of thirst and holds out his hands, desperate for water. That is the sort of longing the psalmist seems to communicate here. He *needs* the salvation, promise, and comfort from God that he mentions in these verses.

Then he uses interesting imagery in the next verse, 83: "I have become like a wineskin in the smoke." Probably not imagery you have used recently! The imagery may escape us a bit, but our inevitable reaction to it is that it cannot be good. The psalmist may want us to think of some kind of leather pouch. It has smoke damage, so perhaps it has been sitting under a fire. This leather pouch is dried and cracked. It may well be useless. Whatever exactly this imagery communicates, the psalmist presents himself in pitiful condition. He feels dried up and good for nothing.

Next the psalmist speaks about his enemies. Such reflection on his enemies—the enemies of the faith—appears repeatedly in Psalm 119. Verses 84 and 86 speak of those who persecute him, and he feels the weight of their oppression. In between those verses, verse 85 describes insolent people digging pits for him. It is as if they know where he takes his morning walk, and they dig a hole out in front of him so that he will fall into it.

Verse 87 points to the result of all this oppression: "They have almost made an end of me on earth." The psalmist's very life is in danger. He feels like he is on the brink of death.

But it is interesting, in this stanza, that these oppressors are not the only ones the psalmist is concerned about. The psalmist also has a complaint against God himself. This ratchets up the stanza's intensity yet another notch. The psalmist asks God multiple questions. Back to verse 82: "I ask, 'When will you comfort me?'" Then in verse 84: "How long must your servant endure? When will you judge those who persecute me?" Finally, in verse 86 he lifts a plea to God: "They persecute me with falsehood; help me." It's as if the psalmist is telling God that he could prevent all this. If God would just step up, help him, and destroy his enemies, the psalmist would not face these extreme hardships. As he sees his life ebbing away, he feels so much distress that he dares to suggest that God is tardy in answering him. The final verse of the stanza, 88, echoes the psalmist's fear of imminent death: "In your steadfast love give me life."

As we think about this stanza—which, as I mentioned, could be the most despairing stanza in this psalm—let us remember the amazing good news that we saw in the previous two stanzas: God rescues his people from judgment. Judgment is never his last word to us. But that does not mean believers are free from hardship, even serious hardship. Our psalmist was a justified believer delivered from coming wrath, but God called him to continue suffering. We need to linger here for a moment because it is so important. Many false teachers promote spiritually harmful ideas related to this topic. Allegedly Christian teachers say that if we are obedient and faithful, and if we pray in the right way, God will prosper us in this life. This is simply a lie. Yet even if we know it is false we can be tempted to think in these ways, however subtly. When we face trials or when God deprives us of something valuable, we think: "Has God abandoned me? Have I done something wrong? Is God judging me? If I had acted better, would I have avoided this?" But that is not how Christianity works.

Sometimes Christians feel like wineskins in the smoke. This may not be the imagery that comes immediately to mind, but it surely resonates with many Christians as they read it. Yet in the big picture, feeling like a wineskin in the smoke is not a sign that something is wrong. In the smaller picture, of course something is wrong—there is nothing normal about sin, evil, or being put to shame. But in the big picture, God has told us ahead of time and prepared us for trials in life. There will be times when we will look in the mirror and see a wineskin in the smoke. What sustains us then? In part, what sustains us is the good news considered in the previous two stanzas: the deliverance God provides through Christ, who by the cross endured God's ultimate judgment on our behalf.

The psalmist, however, in the next stanza provides another way to look at things and thus another source of encouragement. I suppose this is one of the benefits of a long psalm: it allows us the opportunity to explore spiritual realities from different angles. So we turn to this next stanza, with its radical turn of perspective from the depths of despair to some of the most exalted language in the psalm.

* * * * *

In the first three verses of Lamed, verses 89-91, the psalmist identifies several things that are lasting and firm. The first, in verse 89, is God's word: "Forever, O LORD, your word is firmly fixed in the heavens." It might seem odd initially that this psalmist would speak of God's word as fixed in heaven. Don't we have God's word before us in the pages of Scripture? What good would it do us to have God's word up in heaven? But in our own experience, what is more fixed than the heavens above? So much is unpredictable in our world. So much is unstable: pandemics, economic shocks, and political shakeups surprise and dismay us. Yet the stars above do not change. Of course, the skies look a little different every night, but that is predictable. Competent astronomers can tell us far in advance on which days stars will appear or planets align. Thus, the psalmist's statement that God's "word is fixed in the heavens" is quite remarkable. The Scriptures are as certain, firm, and predictable as the heavens above. They are as fixed as the stars. Scripture uses this powerful metaphor elsewhere too. In both Jeremiah 31 and 33, for example, the prophet constructed a similar analogy to explain that if God is faithful to the covenant he made with the day and night and with the stars above, he will also surely be faithful to the covenant he made with David his servant. The heavens above are fixed, and you see God's faithfulness in sustaining them. How much more with his word and with the covenants he has made with his people?

Verse 90 mentions the second thing that is firm and fixed, and that is God's faithfulness: "Your faithfulness endures to all generations." Note the logic the psalmist follows. If God's word is fixed forever, then surely his faithfulness is fixed as well, because his word promises that he shall be faithful to his people. So if his word endures forever, his faithfulness must as well. We can count on it, even as we can count on the stars above remaining firm and fixed.

Next, the second part of verse 90 states: "You have established the earth, and it stands fast." The psalmist has spoken of the heavens being fixed and now he writes something similar about the earth. Of course, the earth sometimes moves. Earthquakes are dangerous events. Even so, in our experience, the earth really is stable and predictable. Rivers and mountains endure for millennia while nations rise and fall around them. So verse 90 reinforces the psalmist's claim about God's faithfulness. If God established the earth and it stands fast, how much more will God preserve and protect his people, to whom he has made such great and precious promises?

Verse 91 sums it up: "By your appointment they stand this day, for all things are your servants." The heavens, the earth, God's word, God's people—are all under God's command. They are all servants of God. And because God is faithful to his promises, they all stand fast before him.

In verses 92-93, the psalmist considers how this endurance of God's word sustains his people. He focuses on how the fixedness of his word is of great benefit and encouragement to us when all is changing around us. Verse 92 returns to an idea the psalmist has utilized before, that of delighting in God's law: "If your law had not been my delight, I would have perished in my affliction." The idea of affliction is a familiar one too by now in Psalm 119. In preceding stanzas, the psalmist described his past affliction and his repentance. Now, as he reflects again on this affliction, he explains that he was able to get through it by delighting in God's word. That is not surprising, is it? Think back to the books of the Old Testament law, especially Deuteronomy. Deuteronomy predicted that God would send his people into exile as the ultimate punishment for their rebellion. But it also promised that after this judgment God would remember his promises to Abraham, Isaac, and Jacob and bring his people back to their Promised Land. We can almost picture this psalmist, sitting as a sojourner in his affliction, away from home, and reading such promises in Deuteronomy. God's word assured him that his time of exile was not the end of the story. God's word promised deliverance, and if God's word is fixed in the heavens, then its promise cannot fail.

So how fitting that verse 93 says: "I will never forget your precepts, for by them you have given me life." You may recall that he asked for life at the end of the previous stanza. Now he recognizes that God does this. God had promised, even in the books of the law, to give his people life after exile. God will not forget his promises, and we should not forget them either. We forget a lot of things, and it is just as well, because so many things are not worth remembering. It is not worth cluttering our brains with much of it. But God's word—his faithful, powerful, valuable word—is something to remember.

The psalmist calls us to join him. As we do, let us consider how much greater reason we have for confidence and delight in God's word than even the psalmist had. The psalmist expresses amazing confidence in the word of God throughout this psalm. But we have seen greater things than he and thus should have greater confidence. Think of Paul's words in 2 Corinthians 1. Paul reflected on God's promises of old and said that all those promises are Yes and Amen in Jesus Christ. Christ has fulfilled the multitude of Old Testament promises. New covenant Christians have the full account of that in the New Testament. We know how the story turns out, but this psalmist did not. He had seen some of God's promises fulfilled, but for the most part their fulfillment lay in the future. We have the privilege of embracing those promises as fulfilled in the birth, life, death, and exaltation of our Lord Jesus Christ. How could we ever forget such things? They are truly worth remembering.

The psalmist then continues, in verses 94-95, these wonderful reflections on God and his work for us and the reasons we have to be confident. Verse 94 begins unremarkably. He says: "I am yours." But consider this in light of this stanza thus far. In all the previous verses he ascribes something to God. He has spoken of "your" word, faithfulness, appointment, law, and precepts. And then here in verse 94: "*I* am yours." All these other things are God's. They are fixed and established because they belong to him. They cannot fail. And now the psalmist says that he himself is "yours." Do you see the implications of that? The psalmist is claiming: "I cannot fail. I must endure. I am fixed. I, a wineskin in the smoke, am as fixed as the stars above, because I belong to God. I belong to him because his words make promises to me. God is faithful and that faithfulness will not fail."

Only after saying this does he mention the wicked in verse 95: "The wicked lie in wait to destroy me, but I consider your testimonies." He does not mention the wicked until the second-to-last-verse of this stanza. He mentions them often in this psalm. He mentioned them several times in the previous stanza. But it seems that when he began reflecting on the firmness and fixedness of the word of God, he forgot about the wicked who were pressing in upon him, trying to take his life, and digging pits in front of him. They are off his mind as he focuses on the faithfulness of his God. He does mention them once here, in verse 95, but not with the same sense of desperation or of imminent peril: "The wicked lie in wait to destroy me." That is still true, but he "considers your testimonies." And by this point in the stanza, we know what that means. It means that he is not afraid. He can face these enemies because he knows that he has a sovereign and faithful God who keeps his promises. He can be confident.

Then he ends the stanza on a marvelous note. I think we would be disappointed if this stanza did not end with wonderful imagery and great encouragement for us. And we are not disappointed. He says: "I have seen a limit to all perfection, but your commandment is exceedingly broad." We experience many wonderful and profound things in this world. They give us joy and delight. We can return to them repeatedly and find a sense of satisfaction. In them we get a glimpse of perfection. Maybe a sublime piece of music takes your breath away. You lack words to describe it. But whatever it is that seems to approach perfection in this life, the psalmist reminds us that it still has limits. If you listen to the most beautiful piece of music over and over and over again, you will eventually get sick of it. The food that gives you the most delight will stop delighting you if you over-indulge. Eventually we find limits to all the apparently perfect things in this world. Yet God's word, the psalmist says, "is exceedingly broad."

God's word is not like these other things. You can see a limit to their perfection, but you will never, ever plumb the depths of the Scriptures. You will never reach the end of its perfection. You can read God's word over and over again—and you should—and you will never exhaust its riches. It never fails to give new encouragement, new consolation, and new and wonderful ways to experience the promise, grace, and mercy of our God. Sin as you might, fail as you might—God's faithfulness will never lose its power.

When the psalmist calls Scripture "exceedingly broad" it is as if he asks us to look as far as we can. Look as far as you can to the east and then to the west. Just try. Perhaps you have been out somewhere, maybe in the central United States, where there are not mountains or human development. You look as far as you can in every direction and you cannot see a limit. The horizon in one direction seems to go on forever and it is the same in the other direction. The psalmist suggests that this is what God's word is like. As deeply as you study it, you will never bump up against the limits of its perfection—nor the perfection of God's faithfulness and love for you. It is an endless horizon.

In those trials depicted in the first of our two stanzas, may you be encouraged by the fact that God's love and comfort for you through his word have no limits. They are indeed exceedingly broad.

7

Wiser than My Enemies

Psalm 119:97-112

Psalm 119 is one of the more memorable parts of Scripture. Here, in the middle of our Bibles, lies a very long text. Christians have called it the Great Psalm or the Long Psalm, and that's exactly what it is. It is the single longest chapter in Scripture. Psalm 119 is perhaps best known for its use of different terms to speak of God's word. Almost every verse says something about it. The psalm expresses how wonderful, profound, comforting, and instructive God's word is. Thus, Psalm 119 has a special place in the hearts of God's people and in the life of his church.

At the same time, reading and understanding Psalm 119 presents difficulties. If you have ever tried to read it through all at once, you may not have made it. Among the challenges of reading Psalm 119 is that we do not know the specific context in which the psalmist wrote it. We wonder about our psalmist's situation as he wrote these profound words.

The author does give us some clues. One helpful clue for understanding the psalm is that he is a *sojourner*. He is away from home, unsettled in this world. Telling us that he is a sojourner is to use a loaded term, because it is an important word in Scripture. Genesis applies the term many times to Abraham. Yet many years later, when God brought his people Israel into the Promised Land under Joshua, they were no longer sojourners. God gave them a home. They were settled.

Nevertheless, God told them in the law of Moses that he would judge them if they rebelled against him, and the worst of the judgments that he threatened was to expel them from the land. He would make them live among Gentile nations again. In other words, he would make them sojourners once more. So, when the psalmist tells us he is a sojourner, we ought to pay attention. It is a signal that something has gone wrong. Our psalmist, and perhaps God's people as a whole, have been rebellious and God has driven them from their land. Perhaps the psalmist is one of the Babylonian exiles. This background explains why the psalmist so often confesses his sin, expresses distress at his great affliction, and cries out to God for deliverance.

Our sojourning psalmist has a rough life, but you would not know it by reading the first ten verses of our text, the Mem and Nun stanzas. It is as if the psalmist's troubles have melted away. Our psalmist reflects on how things ought to be, rather than how things are. But then a few verses into the Nun stanza the psalmist awakens back into reality. He remembers that things are not as they ought to be. He is still a suffering sojourner. Yet the psalmist does not lose hope. He knows that the afflictions he suffers as a sojourner are not the end of the story. God is still his hope and his inheritance. He knows that the way things ought to be will come true one day.

* * * * *

One interesting thing about Psalm 119 you may have noticed, if you have studied it, is that its mood goes up and down. At some points the psalmist sinks to great depths and unveils the anguish of his heart. At other times he rises to the peaks of exaltation, praising and rejoicing in the Lord. The Kaph stanza, two stanzas prior to where we begin here, is perhaps the lowest point of the psalm. Then the following Lamed stanza, immediately preceding our text, rises again to the heights of confidence. I point that out because the psalmist ended the previous stanza with this grand statement: "I have seen a limit to all perfection, but your commandment is exceedingly broad." The psalmist seems to reflect on his experience in the world, in which he has tasted excellent things that approach perfection. But he has found that nothing is perfect. Everything has its limits. But not God's word. It is exceedingly broad. You can read Scripture once or ten times or a thousand times and it will never lose its power. It will never cease to instruct and encourage you.

Our text begins immediately after this. Verse 97 states: "Oh how I love your law." The psalmist picks right up where he left off. At the end of the previous stanza the psalmist was lost in admiration and wonder at God's word, and now he proceeds to profess his love for God's word. The movement of his heart should make sense to us as human beings. We begin with fascination and admiration toward something or someone and we end up falling in love. For the psalmist, it was similar with God's word. How can we not love something that is so marvelous?

In the second part of this opening verse, 97, the psalmist adds: "It is my meditation all the day." The psalmist loves God's word, and that is not simply a feeling. True love brings forth action. If you tell your spouse and children, "I love you," but you are uninterested in them, they will not think your profession of love is sincere. If we truly love the word of God, whose perfection has no limit, how can we not ponder it intensely? God's word does not demand admiration from a distance but constant meditation.

In Colossians 3, Paul says to every Christian—not only to pastors or theologians, but to every Christian—"Let the word of Christ dwell in your hearts richly." This sounds like what our psalmist is saying. And if the psalmist so loved God's word, despite having only a part of the Old Testament as we know it, how much more for us? We have the entirety of the Old Testament and the full revelation of the New Testament. God's word should be even more wonderful to us, and we should thus love it more dearly. It deserves the meditations of our heart.

And as the next two verses make clear, doing so brings great benefit. We should not love God's word merely to get good things in return, but we get them nonetheless. First, the psalmist says in verse 98: "Your commandment makes me wiser than my enemies." Maybe that seems obvious, but let us think about it for a moment. Many enemies of God's people are very smart, accomplished, and successful. Yet this verse reminds us that the humblest Christian who hears, reads, and meditates on God's word has a wisdom surpassing that of the most intelligent, accomplished unbeliever. That is because the word of God informs us of things about God, ourselves, and this world that unbelievers have no access to—in fact, it informs us of the most important things about God, ourselves, and this world. The word communicates wisdom that makes us wiser than our enemies. That should be an encouragement to us.

Verses 99-100 may not seem so obvious: "I have more understanding than all my teachers…. I understand more than the aged," or, more than the elders. That may cause you to raise your eyebrows a bit. What would you think about a student who said: "Oh, I'm smarter than all my teachers?" What would you think about a member of your church who said: "I'm wiser than all the elders of this congregation?" That sounds arrogant. So what is the psalmist telling us? The psalmist could be reflecting on a deficiency in his education as a youth. This would be striking since the psalmist was well-educated by the standards of his day. After all, he wrote a long, beautiful, literarily sophisticated poem! Plus, certain features of Psalm 119 suggest that its author may have been a king. This would give even more reason to think he was well-educated. Yet this psalmist had been driven from the Promised Land and become a sojourner. He lived during a time of rebellion among God's people. Perhaps he looked back at his education, as good as it must have been in some ways, and realized that his teachers did not truly honor and elucidate God's word. And thus his dedication to Scripture makes him wiser than these teachers.

Or perhaps the psalmist was reflecting on the fact that no matter how good human teaching is—or preaching, for that matter—it is never better than God's word itself. God wills that there be preachers and teachers to instruct his people in the word. But no Christian preacher has ever delivered a sermon that was better than the text he was preaching. God's word has a power that not even the most eloquent teacher or preacher can match. God's word itself, as the power of God unto salvation, radiates wisdom and understanding. And that is why Christians should not be followers of men. We must not follow the way of this world and love celebrity—celebrity teachers, preachers, or writers. We are only devotees of the word of God, and we accept with gratitude those who humbly minister it to us.

Note one other thing in verse 100: "I understand more than the aged, for I keep your precepts." The psalmist spoke earlier about *meditating* on the word of God all the day. But here he says he has understanding because he *keeps* God' precepts. Ultimately, we cannot understand the word of God unless we are living it. We do not merely hear it but also put it into practice. This is the only way to understand the Scriptures in their fullness.

It thus follows that in these next two verses, 100 and 101, the psalmist describes how he holds back his feet from every evil way and does not turn aside from God's rules. He recognizes the necessity of walking according to the ways of the word. And as he does, it prompts this beautiful statement in verse 103: "How sweet are your words to my taste, sweeter than honey to my mouth." Here the psalmist delights in God's word. What a marvelous progression in the psalmist's thought. At the end of the previous stanza he expressed wonder and admiration for God's word. He began our stanza talking about his love for God's word. And now at the end of the stanza, he speaks of his joy in God's word. This is how it works in ordinary human experience. We love what we admire, and we take delight in what we love. This is also how it works with the word of God. We don't only love it, but we also rejoice in it. Its wisdom, illumination, comfort, and encouragement delight us.

The stanza closes with verse 104: "Through your precepts I get understanding; therefore I hate every false way." We have seen the logical progression as the psalmist takes us from wonder to love to joy. So perhaps we don't expect him to speak of hatred. Yet there is a logic here as well, isn't there? If we really love and delight in the truth of God's word, how can we not hate what is false? So often our sinful hearts do not hate evil the way we should. Evil things fascinate us, and we play with them in our minds instead of banishing them. Thus, as we ask the Lord for strength to love and rejoice in his word, let us also ask for a genuine hatred of what is evil. May we never delight in that.

* * * * *

There is no break in the action as our second stanza begins. The opening of Nun stays on the same trajectory we have been following in Mem. Verse 105 could be the best-known individual verse of Psalm 119: "Your word is a lamp to my feet and a light to my path." This fits so well into the psalmist's train of thought. Throughout Scripture, the ideas of truth and light often go together. The Gospel of John provides powerful examples. Since God's word brings truth, wisdom, and understanding, according to the previous stanza, the psalmist naturally speaks of God's word as a light and lamp, showing us the way to walk.

The next verse, 106, says: "I have sworn an oath and confirmed it, to keep your righteous rules." The fact that the psalmist takes an oath is quite interesting. Oath-taking was a common feature of Old Testament religion. The Mosaic law had many regulations about taking oaths—and about taking vows, which are similar but not the same. The psalmist's oath should get our attention because oath-taking was one of the most serious things an old covenant Israelite could do. In an oath, a person took God's name upon his lips and made a solemn commitment. He called down a curse upon his head if he did not do what he swore. We can understand why the author of Ecclesiastes 5 mused that it is better to keep silent than to take a vow and not keep it.

Let us pause here for a moment and reflect on what the psalmist is doing. He takes an oath and he *confirms* it. Confirming an oath is serious business too. Some kinds of oaths or vows that one could take under the law of Moses required confirmation to be binding. For example, if a young girl took an oath, it was not binding for her until her father confirmed it. It is doubtful that the psalmist swore an oath that needed confirmation, so the fact that he confirmed it is even more striking. He wanted to leave no doubt that he meant it. And what he committed himself to do was to keep God's righteous rules. He took God's name on his lips and bound himself to observe his law. We cannot help but ask: can the psalmist really keep this oath? He has confessed his rebellion against God earlier in Psalm 119, so we know he is a sinner. He is a repentant sinner, but a sinner, nonetheless. And yet he swears an oath to keep God's law. How will this turn out?

To address this question, consider that these first ten verses of our text—the eight verses of Mem and first two verses of Nun—

stand out in Psalm 119. We get the impression that the psalmist has completely forgotten his present circumstances. He reflects on how things ought to be. Throughout the rest of the psalm, the psalmist constantly reflects on his afflictions and on the wicked people persecuting him. He constantly cries out to God for help. None of this appears in these ten verses. He does not mention his enemies or his afflictions. He does not offer a single prayer to God. This is why I suggest that he is reflecting on how things ought to be.

If he was indeed a king, or had been king, he may be speaking about how he should have acted as ruler of God's people. Consider Deuteronomy 17. God commanded that when Israel appointed a king, the king must have a copy of God's law by his side, read it, and live by it. It sounds like these verses we have considered thus far, doesn't it? Or consider King Solomon, the wisest man on earth. The verses of our text thus far describe someone who sounds a lot like Solomon. He was certainly wiser than his enemies, his teachers, and his elders. We might even consider David, that great king of Israel. Only a few psalms ahead in your Bibles, Psalm 132 describes an oath that David took. He swears to God that he will not rest until he finds a dwelling place for the ark of the Lord. That is what the kings of Israel were supposed to do: be committed to God's word, to excel in wisdom, and to take oaths and keep them. If they did, God had promised to bless his people. They would dwell securely in their land.

Once our psalmist gets to this point, however, it is as if reality comes crashing down upon him. In the following verses, 107-110, all the things I told you were absent from the previous ten verses appear again in abundance. Once again he writes about how afflicted he is and about the wicked people laying snares for him. In verses 107 and 108 alone he offers three prayers to God, asking for help. The psalmist who has been dreaming of how things ought to be now opens his eyes and remembers that things are not as they ought to be. He wrestles again with the fact that he is a suffering sojourner.

Of course, no king of Israel ever lived up to the high standard of Deuteronomy 17. Even David, the man after God's own heart, could not complete the task he swore to do in Psalm 132. He did not build a temple for the ark of the Lord. Solomon excelled in wisdom and yet fell into folly later in life. Even the greatest kings of Israel failed, and God therefore brought terrible judgments upon Israel.

Nevertheless, it is remarkable what we find in the last two verses of the Nun stanza. We might expect this psalmist to be discouraged. But instead he is full of hope and joy in the Lord. True, things are not as they ought to be. But the psalmist seems to hang on to those meditations about how things ought to be and turn them into a prophecy of the future, of how things will be one day. In verse 111 he says: "Your testimonies are my heritage forever." Our psalmist is a sojourner who has been driven from his inheritance in the Promised Land. Yet he remains confident that he still has a heritage—that is, an inheritance. God has not disinherited him permanently. Sojourning is not the end of the story. God's word has given him this confidence, and thus he adds in verse 111 that God's word is the joy of his heart.

Finally, in verse 112 he states that he is inclined to perform God's statutes forever. He uses the term "forever" twice in these last two verses. He also adds "to the end" in verse 112. Though sojourning now, he had a wonderful inheritance from the Lord that would endure.

* * * * *

Although no king of Israel to that point had been the kind of king that he describes, or that Deuteronomy 17 describes, the psalmist was confident that one was coming. We praise God that he has indeed sent our Lord Jesus Christ, the great son of David.

He had the word of God in his heart. Even when he went to the temple at the age of twelve, he was wiser than his teachers and elders. He was not only a little wise. He was the very wisdom of God, revealed to us. He also swore and kept his oaths. Hebrews 10, quoting Psalm 40, states that when Jesus came into the world, he said, "I have come to do your will, O God"—and he completed it. Through him, our rebellion has been forgiven, our curse lifted, and our inheritance won.

One of the reasons Psalm 119 speaks so powerfully to us as new covenant Christians is that we, like the psalmist, are sojourners. That means we are away from our true home, our heavenly inheritance. It also means that we will have troubles and afflictions in this world. Wicked people persecute Christians. Despite our very different cultural and historical contexts from the psalmist's, his sufferings really are not foreign to us. And like the psalmist we can be confident and joyful in the word of God, which promises us an inheritance. Indeed, we should be much more confident and joyful than the psalmist, for we have much more of the Scriptures than he did and understand God's plans for us so much more deeply. Let us join the psalmist in confessing that we have a heritage forever. As Paul said in Romans 8, we are "heirs of God and fellow heirs with Christ, provided we suffer with him in order that we may also be glorified with him." May that give us profound encouragement during the afflictions of this present age.

8

Time for Judgment

Psalm 119:113-128

Although this psalmist does not tell us his name or when he lived, we learn some important things about him as we read the psalm. One of them is that he is a sojourner. The book of Genesis repeatedly calls Abraham a sojourner. This is because he had no permanent home but wandered from place to place, living in tents. But after God brought his people out of Egypt, he settled them in the Promised Land and gave them a permanent place to live. He gave them this land as an inheritance, and that was a very big deal. He gave an inheritance of land to tribes, clans, and particular families. They were to live in their inheritance from generation to generation and not sell it to others. This was God's pledge of a greater, everlasting inheritance to come.

Yet when God gave Israel the law of Moses, he warned them that if they rebelled he would drive them out of this land. They would go to live in the land of others—of pagan Gentiles. And that is how it turned out. So when this psalmist tells us that he is a sojourner, we know that affairs have gone badly for Israel.

To be driven from the Promised Land and made a sojourner in the land of God's enemies was the curse and judgment of God. Perhaps our psalmist was one of the exiles in Babylon. He has told us by this point in Psalm 119 that he was a sinner who went astray. He had repented and was restored in his relationship to God, but he was still living in a foreign land. Thus, he was surrounded by enemies of God, and that made life very difficult for him.

The New Testament tells us that Christians are sojourners and exiles in this world. It is not because we have been driven from an earthly promised land. Some Christians are political exiles, but most of us are not. We are sojourners and exiles because our citizenship is in heaven, as Philippians 3 puts it. Here we have no lasting city, but we seek a city to come, according to Hebrews 13. So as long as we live in this world, we are spiritual sojourners and exiles. We live among people, many of whom hate the Christian religion and hate the name of Christ. This is one of the reasons why Psalm 119 has so often resonated with new covenant Christians. This Old Testament psalmist knew what it was like to be a sojourner in this world, with the various trials and frustrations that they entail.

These matters are important background for the two stanzas before us now, the Samekh and Ayin stanzas, verses 113-128. Throughout this psalm, the author repeatedly reflects on the wicked people among whom he lives and who cause so much trouble for him. But these stanzas focus on these enemies in a special way. The psalmist not only asks for protection against these wicked people but he actually asserts his hatred for them. And this raises some important and difficult questions for us. How do we view the unbelievers among whom we live? What attitude should we have toward those who hate the gospel of Christ?

These stanzas have much to teach us. God still calls us as new covenant believers to love what is good and to hate what is evil, and in fact he has shown us even more wonderful ways to do this than our old covenant psalmist knew.

* * * * *

We look first at the Samekh stanza, which begins in this way: "I hate the double-minded, but I love your law." He pairs love and hatred. Of course, we naturally think of love and hatred together, since they are opposites. The psalmist has played already on this love-and-hatred theme. Just two stanzas earlier, Mem began, in verse 97: "Oh, how I love your law!" And the Mem stanza ended in verse 104: "therefore I hate every false way." The psalmist was a skilled poet, and the way he structured this previous stanza forces us to think about what we love and what we hate. He brings us back to this issue at the opening of our present stanza, although here he places love and hate right next to each other. In the Mem stanza, he loved God's law and hated false ways. Here at the opening of our text, he states again that he loves God's law. But he says that he hates wicked *people*. It's one thing for our psalmist to say that he hates false *ways*. It's another to say that he hates double-minded *human beings*.

His opening statement may make us uncomfortable. Our Lord Jesus told us, in Matthew 5, that we should *love* our enemies and pray for those who persecute us. Yet here our psalmist proclaims without ambiguity that he hates the double-minded. This should make us curious. How will the psalmist work this out? What's on his mind? We need to keep reading.

In verse 114 he says, talking to God: "You are my hiding place and my shield; I hope in your word." By calling God his hiding place and shield, he thinks about God as his defender. If you want to go on the offensive, you will ask for a sword or a spear. But if you are being attacked, you might look for a hiding place. You might need a shield to defend yourself. Thus, he communicates immediately that these evildoers he hates are attacking him. They are the aggressors. He has not gone after them, but they have come after him. This provides some initial perspective.

Then in the next verse, 115, he says: "Depart from me, you evildoers, that I may keep the commandments of my God." A couple of things to note here. It is unusual in Psalm 119 for the author to address wicked people themselves. He often addresses God, but rarely addresses fellow human beings. But here is an exception. We might even get the sense that he is raising his voice a bit. You do not say "depart from me, evildoers" in a soft, gentle tone. He is rebuking them. He does so because he wants to keep God's commandments. This indicates that these evildoers are not merely inconveniencing him but are also threatening his spiritual health. Somehow they are trying to prevent him from serving his God. So you can see that the stakes are high.

The psalmist addresses God again in verses 116 and 117. He offers up short prayers. Although he does not use many words, he covers a lot of ground. He asks God in verse 116 to uphold him according to his promise, that he might live. He implies that his life is threatened. Then he asks God that he would not be put to shame. The wicked delight in putting God's people to shame by exposing their sins and weaknesses and humiliating them. Next, in verse 117, he requests God to hold him up that he might be safe, so that he would have regard for his statutes continually. The psalmist thus seeks God's help in a number of different ways.

Verses 118 and 119 continue this line of thought as the psalmist considers these evildoers who oppose him. He describes what God does to such evildoers. He does not actually pray that God would take such action but simply states what

God does: "You spurn all who go astray from your statutes, for their cunning is in vain. All the wicked of the earth you discard like dross, therefore I love your testimonies." First, then, God spurns all who go astray from his statutes. When we hear that God spurns evil people, perhaps our minds turn to the second psalm, which says that God laughs at the wicked. Psalm 119 seems to say something similar here. Then the next verse says that God discards all the wicked of the earth like dross. In effect, God throws out the wicked as if they are worthless garbage. Then the psalmist concludes: "Therefore I love your testimonies." The psalmist delights in the fact that God despises the wicked and casts them out. The psalmist delights in the judgment of God against the wicked—that is, the wicked people he said he hated at the beginning of the stanza.

Let's take stock of what our psalmist has said. Should our attitude toward the wicked be the same as his? As I mentioned, our Lord Jesus Christ was very clear in the New Testament that we should love our enemies. Under the old covenant law of Moses, God called his people to wage holy war against their Gentile pagan neighbors in the land of Canaan. Our Lord Jesus gave us no such command in the New Testament. We are not to wield the sword against unbelievers. We even should love our enemies. One of the things the Samekh stanza of Psalm 119 helps us realize is how difficult those commands of our Lord Jesus Christ really are. If we love the Lord and love his word— which the psalmist places before us in the first verse of our stanza—it is perfectly natural to hate those who oppose God and his word and who try to destroy his people. In important respects, the hatred the psalmist expresses is the obvious and appropriate attitude. If we do not hate evil—that is, if we lack an inner passion to oppose what is false and wicked—we might ask ourselves whether we really love the Lord and his word. As sinners, we tend to be all too indulgent with evil. We tend to harbor soft spots in our heart for sin. The more we love the Lord, the more we should hate wickedness.

Yet the Lord Jesus has called us to love our enemies. That is truly difficult. Why has God called us to do this? For the moment I will only say this: Jesus commanded us to love our enemies and pray for those who persecute us in the Gospel of Matthew, and it is no coincidence that Matthew ends with the Great Commission: Go into all the world and make disciples of all nations. One basic reason why we should love our enemies and lay down the sword against them is because we cannot evangelize people we have killed! Or to put it less violently: you really cannot proclaim the gospel to someone you hate. Our Lord calls us to lay down our sword and our hatred towards enemies of the gospel so that the gospel might call even these enemies to faith and repentance.

I will come back to these thoughts later. But now let us return to our text. I left off before getting to the last verse of the stanza. Did you notice how it ends in verse 120? The psalmist makes an abrupt turn. This is a characteristic of Psalm 119. One of the advantages of studying it as a single psalm, rather than only reading individual verses, is that you notice such abrupt transitions. The first seven verses of the stanza follow a clear logic. It is easy to understand the case the psalmist is building against the wicked and the delight he feels in God's judgment against them. Then suddenly he says in verse 120: "My flesh trembles for fear of you, and I am afraid of your judgments." How different that sounds from the previous seven verses! The psalmist first delights in God's judgment against the wicked, and then says abruptly that he himself is afraid of God's judgments. The psalmist has been contemplating the wickedness of these evil people, but then, it seems, he looks at his own heart. He recognizes that he is a sinner, as he has confessed earlier in the psalm. It's easy for believers to be offended by the wickedness of this world and to despise the wicked. It is much harder, yet so necessary, for us to examine our own hearts and consciences. What we find may not be very attractive. This is surely why our psalmist writes what he does at the end of this stanza: O Lord, "my flesh trembles for fear of you, and I am afraid of your judgments."

* * * * *

Because the previous stanza ends on a rather uncertain note, we are curious to see how the psalmist proceeds. The beginning of the Ayin stanza, verses 121-128, makes clear that the psalmist has not left his train of thought. He continues to reflect on the judgment of God, with respect to both unbelievers and himself.

He begins in verse 121: "I have done what is just and right; do not leave me to my oppressors." He has confessed his fear of God's judgments, in light of his own failings. So it is interesting that the first thing he does here is appeal to his own righteousness. That may not immediately strike us as the right thing to do! But the psalmist, although he is a sinner, is not identical to the wicked people he was talking about through most of the previous stanza. He is not like them. They hate God and his word. They have no interest in repenting. Our psalmist is a sinner too, but he loves the Lord and has repented of his sin. He looks to God's word for encouragement and hope. That distinguishes him radically from the wicked. He appeals to this before God, and we can be sure that God acknowledges it. God knows the difference between his repentant people and unrepentant unbelievers.

But lest we think that the psalmist is actually trusting in his own righteousness for salvation, the next verses make clear this is not the case. He says in verses 122: "Give your servant a pledge of good; let not the insolent oppress me." He humbles himself. He calls himself God's servant. He does not exalt his own righteousness. He asks God to give him a pledge of what is good. He knows that he needs a gift of God. That is how he shall be secure and safe from the divine judgment. God must give him his own pledge. We do not know what the psalmist had in mind, if anything in particular. He had been deprived of the ordinary comforts and encouragements of the old covenant, for God had cast him out of the Promised Land and made him a sojourner. But how marvelously God answered the prayer of this old covenant saint to give him a pledge of good.

God has not ceased to give his people such pledges. For example, consider the way Hebrews 7 speaks of our Lord Jesus Christ as the *surety* of the new and better covenant. This is the only time the New Testament calls Jesus a surety, yet it is one of the most wonderful titles Scripture gives him. We have suretyship in our legal systems still today. A surety is one who guarantees the performance of someone else's responsibilities and the payment of someone else's debts. A surety is precisely what the Lord Jesus Christ is for us. He has taken on our responsibilities and paid our debts. He is a pledge before God. If we claim this surety, we can be confident that none of our responsibilities remains unperformed before the Lord. No debt is left unpaid.

The New Testament also says that the Holy Spirit is a *seal* of our redemption. That is another way of saying that he is a pledge, a promise from God. If you are sealed with the Holy Spirit, God has put an indelible mark on you. The Spirit is a pledge from the Lord that you are his and have an everlasting inheritance. By sealing our redemption, the sacraments of baptism and the Lord's Supper are also divine pledges.

The psalmist continues this line of thought in verse 123: "My eyes long for your salvation and for the fulfillment of your righteous promise." Again, the psalmist is not trusting in his own righteousness. He looks for *God's* salvation. God has made promises to him and he expects their fulfillment. Then verse 124: "Deal with your servant according to your steadfast love." The Old Testament as a whole appeals to God's *steadfast love* repeatedly. There are different ways to translate this Hebrew word—if not steadfast love, perhaps covenant faithfulness or lovingkindness—but we get the meaning. God is our covenant God. He has made commitments to us. And in his love and faithfulness he will not fail to keep all the things he has promised. The psalmist forsakes trust in his own righteousness and rests in the steadfast love of his God. Finally, in verse 125, he again humbles himself and calls himself God's servant. He asks God for understanding that he may know his testimonies. If the psalmist is to be wise, God must teach him.

Let me summarize what the psalmist has done in these opening five verses of the stanza. After expressing fear of God's judgment at the end of the previous stanza, he has proclaimed—or perhaps we might say, preached to himself— the righteousness, steadfast love, and salvation of God. It has restored his confidence. He is not the same as these wicked who will fall under God's judgment. God has promised and pledged salvation to his people.

If we are in any doubt that the psalmist's spiritual confidence has returned, we can just read the next verse, 126: "It is time for the LORD to act, for your law has been broken." That's quite a bold statement. The psalmist speaks as though he is keeping God's schedule and knows it better than God himself does. Statements like this appear elsewhere in the psalms. One of my favorites is Psalm 74:10-11: "How long, O God, is the foe to scoff? Is the enemy to revile your name forever? Why do you hold back your hand, your right hand? Take it from the fold of your garment and destroy them!" To put it in contemporary language, the psalmist tells God to take his hands out of his pockets and destroy the wicked. Our psalmist speaks similarly in Psalm 119. He looks at these wicked people doing terrible things, oppressing God's people, and he cannot wait for God's deliverance any longer. It is as if he looks at his watch and tells God: "It's time!"

We may wonder whether this is an expression of godly hope or one of impatience. Is it presumptuous to talk to God in this way? In the New Testament there seems to be a very fine line between impatience and persistence. The New Testament urges us to be persistent in approaching God and requesting things from him—even demanding things from God, as long as they are according to his will.

Think of Luke 18, which opens with the parable of the unjust judge. A widow keeps going back to a wicked judge, and because she repeatedly asks for justice, finally the judge gets sick of her and gives her what she wants. Luke writes that Jesus told this parable to instruct us that we should pray and not give up. If you can persuade an unjust judge to give you justice simply by bothering him long enough, how much more with our loving heavenly Father, who actually cares about us and wants our good? We should pray and not give up. And one of the things we pray for, as we see in 1 Corinthians 16 and Revelation 22, is that Jesus would come again. "Come, O Lord"—that sounds like a demand. We do not ask it gently. We demand that our Lord should come again. "Come quickly, Lord Jesus."

That prayer is quite similar to our psalmist's. In both cases, we and the psalmist pray: "Come and judge the wicked! Come and make right what's wrong! Come and vindicate your persecuted people!" We should long for that and pray for that. Yet we must do so with godly patience. As 2 Peter 3 reminds us, the Lord is not slow in keeping his promises but he wants all to repent. We can pray "Lord Jesus, come" because God has promised that the Lord Jesus is coming. We pray for what he has told us to pray for, but we remember that his seeming delay is actually a concern for the salvation of all his people.

We must keep both of these things before us. We pray that the Lord would come and make all things right. Yet we are glad for the Lord's patience. We are glad, as Paul says in 2 Corinthians 6, that it's still the "favorable time," the "day of salvation." That means God still holds out the gospel to sinners. Hence Paul also said in that text: "be reconciled to God." There is still time. What if the Lord's patience had run out before you had confessed the name of Christ? And so we are patient, grateful for the Lord's mercy and holding out the gospel, even while we pray: "Come, Lord Jesus." And we know that our Lord knows exactly the right time to do so.

In the last two verses, the psalmist turns back to the themes of love and hate, exactly where our text began. Verse 127 reads: "Therefore, I love your commandments above gold, above fine gold." He picks up an idea from earlier in the psalm. God's word is so precious that it is more valuable than gold. And verse 128: "Therefore I consider all your precepts to be right; I hate every false way." Here he speaks not of hating *people*, as at the beginning of our text, but of hating false *ways*, which is how Mem ended several stanzas back.

* * * * *

Maybe that is a good place for us to conclude as well. God calls us to love the Lord and his word and all the truth it proclaims. He also calls us to hate every false way. We should love and hate the appropriate things even more intensely than the old covenant psalmist loved and hated them, for God has revealed to us so much more of his word and ways.

We may wonder at times how we can both hate what is evil and love our enemies, or how the church, as it proclaims the gospel, can both delight in God's patience and also long for

Christ to come again. This tension will remain with us until that day of Christ's return. But whether the Lord delays his coming for many centuries or comes in our own day, we trust that the Lord's timing is good. Either way, the Lord triumphs. While we wait for Christ, there is nothing the devil hates more than when sinners believe and repent. Do you want to show your hatred for evil? Then promote the ministry of the gospel, for every time the gospel is preached and a sinner turns to Christ, the devil and his kingdom crumble further. If we love the Lord and hate evil, let us hold out that gospel as we also long for the day of Christ's return. He will finish his work. He will put an end to wickedness in this world once and for all.

9

Longing, Sorrow, and Zeal

Psalm 119:129-144

Psalm 119 says much about the word of God. Almost every verse uses a term for God's word. Yet so much more is going on in Psalm 119 than simply telling us about God's word, important as that is. Our psalmist does not mention his name or when he lived in redemptive history, but he tells us much about himself. The Long Psalm opens up his spiritual experience. He tells us about his former rebellion against God and that he became a sojourner, apparently living away from the Promised Land. He also told us that it was good for him to be afflicted by God. He had turned and repented, and he looks again to God in hope. He describes, as well, the deep affliction that confronts him as he continues his sojourn and endures persecution from those who hate God and hate him. Psalm 119 develops so many important themes for our instruction and encouragement.

In the two stanzas before us, the psalmist identifies several emotions he has experienced—or to use older terminology, several passions. All of us have emotions. Emotions or passions are strong feelings that intrude upon us in ways we do not plan and that do not seem fully in our control. It is not bad to have emotions. To have emotions is simply to be human. From one perspective, it is good to have emotions, since God created us as emotional creatures. But the fall into sin has corrupted our emotions, as it has other aspects of our being. We sinners tend to have the wrong emotions at the wrong times. There is nothing wrong *per se* with feeling sadness, happiness, fear, or anger. We can experience all of those righteously. The problem is that we sinners tend to get sad about the wrong things and angry about the wrong things, or to get sad or angry about the right thing but in the wrong way or at the wrong time. Thus, one aspect of the Holy Spirit's work of sanctification is to shape our hearts and minds so that we increasingly experience the right emotions in the varied circumstances of life.

Our two stanzas describe three common human emotions, which our English translation refers to as *longing*, *sorrow*, and *zeal*. The psalmist helps us to see how these can be godly emotions by feeling them toward the right things in the right way. These stanzas remind us that God and his word are wonderful, gracious, and righteous, and this fact cannot leave us unmoved.

* * * * *

We first consider the opening three verses of the Pe stanza, verses 129-131, which describe the first of these three emotions. The psalmist begins with a brief statement: "Your testimonies are wonderful." Note that the psalmist uses "wonderful" in a much more profound sense than we often use the term. "Wonderful" in our everyday speech can simply express that something was nice. A person feeds us a mediocre meal and we say, "Oh, that was wonderful." That does not communicate what the psalmist is expressing. He is not saying, "Lord, your testimonies are pretty good." What he says more literally is: "Your testimonies, O Lord, are full of wonders." The Hebrew term the psalmist uses almost always refers to God himself and his actions. Psalm 72:18 is an example: the Lord alone does wonders! The Lord brought his people out of Egypt. The Lord brought his people into the Promised Land. The Lord raised his Son from the dead. The Lord indeed does wondrous works. Let us stand in amazement at this wonder-working God.

Since the word of God reveals these wonders to us, the psalmist rightly says that his testimonies are wonderful. The Bible is indeed full of wonders. This prompts the psalmist to say: "Therefore my soul keeps them." Once you recognize the wonders of God's word, how better to respond than by striving to live in accord with it. A word that is so wonderful is worth keeping.

The psalmist next writes, in verse 130: "The unfolding of your words gives light; it imparts understanding to the simple." This follows the previous verse so beautifully. Since God's word is full of wonders, what does it do? It gives light. You might imagine yourself in a room with a window, in the middle of the day. But a very effective curtain is keeping the sunlight out. It is very dark in the room and you cannot see anything. Then someone rips open that curtain and light just floods the room. While you could not see anything before, now you can see everything crystal clear.

The psalmist indicates that this is what it is like when God's word confronts you. Apart from the Scriptures, we are so ignorant. We grope around in the dark. Then God's word enters and light fills our minds and hearts. The psalmist refers to the "*unfolding* of your words." This is a simple Hebrew word that means "opening." This is why the analogy of opening a curtain is fitting here. Sometimes we use similar terminology when hearing a sermon or a lecture on God's word. We say, "that preacher really opened God's word to us."

What happens when that occurs? Verse 130 continues: it "imparts understanding to the simple." You might recall the term "simple" from the book of Proverbs. Proverbs introduces us primarily to two kinds of people, the wise and the foolish. But it also speaks of the simple. Proverbs often portrays the simple person as young, who is not yet confirmed as either foolish or wise. The simple person has a lot to learn and could still go in either direction. There is a sense in which all of us remain simple, no matter how old we are, for as long as we are in this world we have more to learn. And how do the simple grow in wisdom and understanding? By the unfolding of God's words. That is crucial for moving from simplicity to wisdom.

After these opening two verses, the psalmist describes the first of the passions I mentioned. Verse 131 states: "I open my mouth and pant, because I long for your commandments." Perhaps you would not list *longing* if I asked you to come up with a short list of emotions. But I think this is an accurate way to describe the psalmist's meaning. We all know what it is to feel a deep desire for something. Deep desires can come upon us suddenly. We experience a craving for an item we see or for an object that comes to mind. Sometimes these things we long for are not good to desire. But other things are worthy of our longing.

The psalmist says that that he longs for God's commandments. God's word is the object of his craving. He depicts himself in a rather unattractive way: "I open my mouth and pant." But this psalmist does not really care about the impression he makes on others. As an animal opens its mouth and pants if it has not had food or water for a long time, and as it deeply desires them—that is how we should be with the word of God. If we are to grow spiritually from simplicity to wisdom, we need the nourishment of Scripture. A young person needs physical nourishment to grow from childhood to adulthood. So also God's people need the nourishment of God's word to grow toward spiritual maturity.

It is interesting to think about how often Scripture uses the metaphor of food to depict God's good gifts. Earlier in Psalm 119, verse 103 states: "How sweet are your words to my taste, sweeter than honey to my mouth." Or you may be familiar with Psalm 81:10, where God says: "Open your mouth wide, and I will fill it." And Jesus declared, in the Sermon on the Mount: "Blessed are those who hunger and thirst for righteousness, for they shall be satisfied." We are fundamentally unsatisfied creatures without God and his kingdom. God has made us for fellowship with himself. That is our highest purpose for existing. As long as we lack the fullness of communion with God, we ought to feel a fundamental longing that calls for satisfaction. As a teenage boy longs for food, so the people of God should long for the spiritual nourishment God's word provides. Let me remind you of one additional text along these lines. In 1 Peter 2, the apostle says: "Like newborn infants, long for the pure spiritual milk, that by it you may grow up into salvation—if indeed you have tasted that the Lord is good."

You do desire things. Human beings inevitably long for satisfaction. Pray that the Lord would work in you a deep desire for the word of God and for the nourishment it brings.

* * * * *

The psalmist describes the second of the emotions we're considering, in verses 132-136—that is, in the final five verses of our first stanza. Of these five verses, four of them are little prayers. The first three verses of the stanza didn't offer any prayers, but these next four do. His turn to prayer makes good sense. The psalmist has recognized his neediness. He longs for nourishment from the word of God. How appropriate, then, that he turns to God and asks for help, for satisfaction of this deep need he knows he has.

The first of these little prayers, in verse 132, reads: "Turn to me and be gracious to me, as is your way with those who love your name." It is a beautiful little prayer. He asks God to turn to him and be gracious to him, and he adds that this is God's way for those who love his name. At first glance there does not seem to be a term for God's word here. However, the Hebrew word translated "way" in the ESV is a term more commonly translated throughout Psalm 119 as "rule" or "judgment." But note here that this refers not to a rule or judgment for *us*. That's how the psalmist usually uses the term. God gives us a rule to follow. But here the psalmist refers to a rule God himself follows. "Way" is not a bad translation. I wonder if an even better term to capture the meaning would be "policy." God has a rule or policy for his own conduct. He has made a judgment about how he will deal with those who love him, that is, his people. The rule or policy is that he turns to them and is gracious to them. If you ask the question "How does God treat his people?" or "What is God's policy for dealing with us?" it is so encouraging to know that God's policy is to turn to us in love and shower us with grace.

Paul puts it in an even more beautiful way in Romans 8:28: God works out all things for the good of those who love him. It's the same idea: for those who love God, God's policy is to turn and be gracious. For those who love God, God works out all things for the good.

The psalmist's second short prayer follows in verse 133: "Keep steady my steps according to your promise, and let no iniquity get dominion over me." The psalmist's spiritual insight is evident here. He is alert to the various dangers we face as sinners. One danger is the evil of our own hearts. As a hymn puts it, "prone to wander, Lord I feel it." So the psalmist asks God to keep his steps steady according to his promise. It is the right request for those tempted to wander. Then he says: "Let no iniquity get dominion over me." He asks that the Lord not let any sin be his master. We should all pray for this, that no sin would exercise lordship over us. Again we might think of Romans. In Romans 6, Paul states that what the psalmist prays for is, in fact, true of everyone who trusts in the Lord Jesus Christ. Paul writes that we are "not under law but under grace," and that therefore "sin will have no dominion over" us. This is a fact for every one of you who trusts in Christ. It does not mean you will not be tempted to sin or will not sin. It means that you, as Christians, have one Lord. You cannot have more than one master, and that is the Lord Jesus Christ. As attractive as some sins may feel and as burdened as we may be by temptations, how encouraging that none of them is our master. Is it not amazing to be able to pray for what God has specifically granted us? We always pray "your will be done," but in cases like this we do not have to wonder what God's will actually is. His will is that sin will not be your master, since you are in Christ.

Then, in verse 134, the psalmist recognizes another spiritual danger, this time not from his own wandering heart but from the outside, from enemies and persecutors: "Redeem me from man's oppression, that I may keep your precepts." This prayer nicely complements the preceding prayer about his internal spiritual life.

Verse 135 is the final of these little prayers: "Make your face shine upon your servant, and teach me your statutes." Hearing this may remind you of a common benediction at the end of worship services. In Numbers 6, the Lord gave Israel what we call the Aaronic blessing: "The LORD bless you and keep you; the LORD make his face to shine upon you and be gracious to you; the LORD lift up his countenance upon you and give you peace." That is a wonderful way to conclude a service, and it is a wonderful way to conclude this series of prayers. Again, the psalmist asks for something the Lord has already promised to give. The Lord declares that his face—his light—shines upon his people. How bold we can be asking for blessings that the Lord has already promised to bestow!

So, the psalmist has offered four prayers and has thereby put several beautiful spiritual truths before us. He now expresses the second of the three emotions in our text. But it may not be the one we would expect after hearing these encouraging four prayers: "My eyes shed streams of tears, because people do not keep your law." The emotion here is *sorrow*. Why is the psalmist sorrowful after delighting in all this grace of God? He tells us why: because people do not keep God's law. There is actually no subject of this last phrase in the original Hebrew. Our translation puts the word "people" in the text because we need a subject in the English language or it does not sound right. But in Hebrew it is merely an understood "they." The psalmist does not identify specifically who it is who do not keep God's law. But he probably refers to fellow Israelites, his brothers and sisters in the covenant community, and not to Gentile pagans. If that is the case, his reaction of sorrow after these four little prayers makes a great deal of sense. He has been reflecting on all the blessings God has given to his people. God has established a policy of turning to his people and being gracious to them. He promises that sin will not have dominion over those who love him. God turns his face and shines upon his people. And how had God's people responded? They had rebelled against God over and over and over again. They had worshiped other gods. They had despised God's goodness. And this fills the psalmist with deep sorrow.

It really is deep sorrow. The psalmist says, literally, that rivers of water are flowing from his eyes. He is not just a little melancholy. It is not merely a little tear that is trickling down his face. No, he is really weeping. Consider Romans again—this time Romans 9, where Paul reflected on old covenant Israel. The psalmist reflected on Israel's rebellion against the Mosaic law, but Paul on their rejection of the Messiah, the Lord Jesus. Paul stated that he had great sorrow and unceasing anguish over Israel. What a tragedy that God's old covenant people had rebelled against him so terribly. But that should also make us contemplate the scandal when God's new covenant people respond in ways similar to old covenant Israel. Of course, God will not end the new covenant in the way that he ended the old covenant. There will not be whole-scale apostasy under the new covenant as there was under the old. Yet we know all too well that new covenant people do many things that bring shame and disgrace upon the name of Christ. God has bestowed so many more blessings upon us than he did upon his people of old. He has revealed so much more of his word. He has done so many more wonderful deeds. Yet how many times—through our failure to love each other or to love our neighbor, through false teaching, or through complaining—do we bring the name of Christ into disgrace? What a tragedy that is! What sorrow it ought to bring from the people of God!

We all get sad. But so many of the things that make us sad, when we stop and think about it, are silly or selfish. Are we truly grieved by our sins—by our own sins and the sins of the people of God? This is what should truly grieve us. The New Testament describes us as a joyful people, and joy should characterize us. Sorrow is not a fruit of the Spirit in Galatians 5, but joy is. Yet there is a kind of sorrow over sin that is compatible with our joy in Christ. Paul explains this in 2 Corinthians 7:10 when he speaks of a sorrow that leads to repentance. That is the sort of sorrow over sin we ought to have. Such sorrow does not keep us in grief but leads us, as individuals and as a church, to repent and be restored in joy. Let us pray for this kind of sorrow.

* * * * *

The third of the three emotions that the psalmist sets before us is in our second stanza, Tsadhe, which we will consider more briefly than the first. A noteworthy feature of this stanza is that the words "righteous" or "righteousness" appear repeatedly in it. It is clear that the psalmist wants these words to stand out and make an impression on us. Since this is the Tsadhe stanza, each verse in the Hebrew begins with the letter Tsadhe, and the words "righteous" and "righteousness" are common Hebrew words beginning with this letter. The psalmist obviously wanted to capitalize on that.

From the outset, the psalmist highlights that God and his word are righteous. What does "righteous" refer to? Think about it along these lines: imagine that there's a standard—a standard of conduct or of right thinking. What is righteous is what is in perfect conformity with that standard. Thus, verses 137 and 138 imply that God and his word conform perfectly to everything that is right. The psalmist returns to this idea several times in the stanza. Everything about God and his word is upright.

Following this introduction to God's righteousness, verse 139 expresses the final emotion we are considering, that is, *zeal*: "My zeal consumes me, because my foes forget your words." What is zeal? Zeal is a sort of eagerness. Zeal is what we feel when some cause captures all of our attention. The world is full of good causes, but we have little time or interest in most of them. Other things distract us. But every so often a cause garners all of our attention and we devote our energy to it, as if nothing else really matters. That is zeal. Our psalmist says that zeal consumes him. That is a good way to speak about zeal. It is like a fire burning within you that needs an outlet.

As with the previous emotions he identified, the psalmist tells us explicitly why he feels the way he does. Zeal consumes him "because my foes forget your words." This statement makes us wonder what its connection is to the theme of *righteousness* that dominates the stanza. The psalmist seems to create a tension for us to wrestle with. He emphasizes that everything about God and his word is perfectly righteous. Yet here he calls our attention to the fact that we live in a world that's full of unrighteousness—specifically, a world full of people who forget God and his word. This is apparently what arouses the zeal of our psalmist. And indeed, how can godly people—when they ponder how righteous God is and how unrighteous the world is—not be filled with a holy zeal to see that remedied?

Before we can think more about our own zeal for God, however, we should remember that God himself has zeal. He especially has zeal to deliver his people from their enemies. The book of Isaiah speaks of this several times. For example, Isaiah 9, a famous prophecy, foretells the coming Messiah, who would be Wonderful Counselor, Mighty God, Everlasting Father, Prince of Peace. Immediately after using these titles for Christ, Isaiah says: "The zeal of the LORD of hosts will do this." God is zealous for saving his people and zealous for sending them a Messiah to accomplish that salvation. So it was no surprise that when Jesus the Messiah came he expressed zeal to do God's work. In John 2, when the disciples saw Jesus clearing the temple, they remembered the Old Testament prophecy: "zeal for your house will consume me." Our Lord was zealous to fulfill the mission for which God sent him: to deliver the people of God.

So we rightly desire to be zealous like our Lord—not for just any cause, but for the cause of Christ's salvation in this unrighteous world. How can we be zealous for God's righteousness? Perhaps Romans tells us what is most important. Romans often uses "righteousness" terminology. Paul explains that the coming of our Lord Jesus Christ was the revelation of God's righteousness. Our Lord Jesus lived a righteous life. And the righteous obedience he accomplished has now been credited to us—imputed to us by faith—so that when God sees us in Christ, he sees us as the righteous.

If you want to be zealous for the righteousness of God in the midst of an unrighteous world, there is nothing simpler and better to do than to believe the gospel of Christ and to promote the preaching of his gospel. Pray for it and support it. For as Christ's gospel is proclaimed, the righteousness of God is revealed, and unrighteous sinners are made righteous by faith. In Galatians 5, Paul also spoke of "the hope of righteousness." Our Lord Jesus will return, and on that day he will put an end to all unrighteousness and establish a perfectly righteous new creation.

I could say more about the remaining verses and how the psalmist revisits the theme of God's righteousness. But I leave you with a call to pray. Pray that the Lord will give you the right sort of zeal. As human beings, we inevitably feel zeal about something or other. Let us pray that the righteousness of God will arouse our zeal more than anything else. Let us pray for the proclamation of the righteousness of God in Christ, as well as for that coming day when he will return, to make all things right at last.

10

The Prayer of the Godly

Psalm 119:145-160

As we see throughout Scripture, prayer has been one of the central practices of God's people in all of history. We who live under the new covenant have special, abounding privileges in prayer that the old covenant saints did not enjoy. Jesus told his disciples, on the night he was betrayed, that they would now pray in his name, which the saints of old had not been able to do. Jesus is in heaven now, praying for us at the right hand of God even as we pray here on earth—another great privilege we have under the new covenant. And since Pentecost, God has poured out the Spirit in full measure upon the people of God, and that Spirit helps us to pray. So we rejoice in the great privileges and power we have in prayer under the new covenant.

Yet there is so much to learn from the Old Testament about prayer. The psalms especially are filled with such instruction. One way to view the psalms is as 150 prayers that show us how to call upon God. Among other things, Psalm 119 is a prayer. But the stanzas we are considering now set prayer before us in a special way. They not only portray the psalmist himself praying but also describe how he prays. He tells us about his own practice and experience of prayer.

As he does, we recognize so much about his experience that is similar to ours today. The psalmist prayed as a sojourner, far away from the Promised Land and from God's temple. The temple in Jerusalem was where God had promised to dwell with his people. But the psalmist was distant from it and had been for a long time. We also know that our psalmist prayed amid deep afflictions. He was a persecuted man. Compare all this to our own situation. We too have a temple, and we also are not there. Our sanctuary is in heaven, where our Savior ministers on our behalf. But we are still on earth. We are also a suffering people. Thus our context in prayer resembles that of the psalmist in many respects. So we can consider this text and see how the psalmist instructs us to pray as a suffering, sojourning people still away from our heavenly temple.

* * * * *

In the opening of the Qoph stanza, the psalmist does not actually do much praying, but he describes his practice of prayer. Notice some of the things he says.

First, notice the verbs he uses in the first two verses, 145 and 146. He does not say "I pray." He could have said that, but instead he writes: "With my whole heart I cry" and "I call to you." I *cry*, I *call*. His use of those verbs depicts prayer as something that emerges from deep within. True prayer does not merely communicate facts to God, or a list of things we are thankful for, or a list of things we want God to do for us this week. Prayer is not like sending God a memo. We call out to God. We cry out to him from our heart. We lay bare our souls before God. That is what prayer is. We all have different personalities and thus have various levels of comfort when laying bare our souls before each other. Some people are very comfortable, it seems, telling anything to anybody. Others of us are very private and jealous to guard the secrets of our hearts. But whatever our personality, there is no point in being a private person before God. God knows what is in our hearts anyway. He knows our deepest thoughts and feelings. We cannot hide anything from God the way we can hide things from our neighbor. Scripture tells us to cast our burdens upon the Lord. In prayer we open ourselves up before the Lord. That should not be embarrassing or shameful. It should be liberating to tell God what he already knows, believing that as we cry out to God, he hears and answers.

So that is one thing these opening verses teach about prayer. Notice also that the psalmist describes prayer as holistic. In verse 145 he says: "With my whole heart I cry." We do not merely pray from the heart, but from our *whole* heart. The psalmist has used this expression previously in Psalm 119. In fact, he used it already in the second verse. There he described his devotion to God with everything that is in him. God's people should not be devoted to their Lord in piecemeal fashion. We do not give a bit of our time and energy to God. Devotion to God should consume us. It is holistic. Back now to verse 145: We should pray with our whole heart. Prayer flows out of holistic devotion to God.

Verses 147-148 present another holistic aspect of prayer. The psalmist cries out to God at all times of the day. He says in verse 147: "I rise before dawn and cry for help." Verse 148 adds: "My eyes are awake before the watches of the night." Whether he is getting up early or staying up late, we find this psalmist at prayer. This may remind us of 1 Thessalonians 5:17, where Paul commanded: "Pray without ceasing." A simple command, but not an easy one. Of course, Paul did not envision conscious prayer for twenty-four hours a day. We have many other responsibilities in life and our minds necessarily focus elsewhere much of the time. But both Paul and our psalmist commended prayer as a way of life for believers. Prayer characterizes Christians. If I asked you to describe someone briefly, you would not pick out something obscure that this person does once in a while. You would pick something typical, something you would expect to see in that person in a casual encounter. It is analogous for prayer with Christians. It characterizes us. This is who we are. Fish swim, birds fly, scorpions sting—and Christians pray. Those who believe in the living God cry out to him day and night.

These opening verses set quite a high bar. They describe prayer as one of our chief characteristics, as it flows from a holistic devotion to the Lord. This description of prayer may even seem a bit intimidating. The next verse, 149, provides wonderful comfort. If we feel any temptation to think that our prayers need to reach a high level of faithfulness, eloquence, or piety before God will hear them, verse 149 sets us straight: "Hear my voice, according to your steadfast love; O LORD, according to your justice give me life." God hears us not because of how much we pray or how profound our prayers are, but because of his *steadfast love*. This translates a common Hebrew term found in the Old Testament. It communicates that God loves us faithfully and keeps his covenant promises. This is why God hears our prayers: because he is faithful and full of tender mercy. As Hebrews 10:20 explains, God in Christ has opened a new and living way for us. Why can we pray? Why are the gates of heaven open to us? Why can we enter God's gates with thanksgiving and his courts with praise? Because Christ has given us access through his broken body and shed blood. We approach the Father in the name of the Son. This is why we know God hears us.

The second phrase in verse 149 asks God to hear because of his *justice*. This may not initially strike us as a good idea! We readily understand that God hears us because of his mercy. But justice? Does not his justice condemn us because of our sin? Yet if you think of this in terms of the work of Christ, the psalmist's appeal makes good sense. If Christ has shed his blood and purchased us with his very life, it would be unjust of God not to hear us. Christ has settled all accounts. We are right with God. And thus it is *just* for God to hear us when we approach him in the name of Christ.

As the psalmist moves to verses 151-152, he does not mention prayer explicitly. But it is easy to see why he says what he does in the context of reflecting on prayer. Remember that we pray out of a deep sense of need. We do not pray because we are strong and can do it ourselves. We pray with a profound sense of weakness, sin, and vulnerability. We also pray with a sense that God is distant from us, in an important sense. God dwells in his heavenly sanctuary. Our Savior, in his resurrected body, is in heaven. He is not here among us. We are away from the Lord, as Paul says in 2 Corinthians 5. We pray with a consciousness of God's distance. So too with our psalmist, who was a sojourner, far away from the temple in Jerusalem. In verse 150 he writes: "They draw near who persecute me with evil purpose." God was distant, in a sense, but who was close to him? Evil people—they seem closer than God, at times. Do you notice how the psalmist plays with the theme of distance and nearness? In verse 150 he says that evildoers are *far* from God's law. And this made their *nearness* to him more troublesome. We pray with the same posture—with a sense of our enemies' proximity. Yet the psalmist says next, in verse 151: "But you are near, O LORD."

Yes, in a sense the Lord is distant. We, like the psalmist, are not in the sanctuary of our God. Yet, as we pray, the Lord draws near to his people. He draws near to us as we call upon his name. We look forward to that day when we will worship God in his presence, face to face with our Lord Jesus Christ. We will not pray in the same way in heaven as we pray now, for then there will be no more sin, no more enemies, and no more distance from our Savior. But even here and now, as we call out to God, we experience our Savior's nearness in a way we do not in any other experience in this life.

This first of our stanzas concludes with two statements about God's word. We can never get away from God's word in Psalm 119! The end of verse 151 reads: "Your commandments are true." Then verse 152: "Long have I known from your testimonies that you have founded them forever." Two great doctrines: God's word is true and God's word is forever. There is a lot of falsehood in this world. So many lies. But God's word is true. And it is not temporary truth. It is not merely truth that is good for me today, while tomorrow something else might be true. No, God's word is forever. It teaches truth that endures, truth we can count on.

* * * * *

We now move to the second stanza before us, Resh. The psalmist has not really gotten prayer out of his head. He does not describe prayer, as he did in the previous stanza. Instead, he prays. He did not offer many prayers *per se* in the previous stanza. But the Resh stanza has many mini prayers. There are several in the opening verses, 153-154: "Look on my affliction and deliver me, for I do not forget your law. Plead my cause and redeem me; give me life according to your promise." We should not miss that the psalmist cries out from a deep sense of need. He says: "Plead my cause"—this is the language of the courtroom. He describes himself as a man on trial and wants God to be his attorney. God must plead his cause. Whether he is in court or if he speaks metaphorically, his situation obviously is not good. He asks God to *redeem* him. To redeem means to purchase, and you need to be purchased if you are a slave. Again, whether this is literal or metaphorical, the psalmist feels oppressed. Then at the end of verse 154 he says: "Give me life." In fact, he asks God to give him life three times in this stanza. One does not keep asking for life unless he feels that death is threatening.

Thus, the psalmist communicates to God the depth of his need. These opening verses of the stanza are not exactly optimistic or cheerful. Verse 155 contributes to this mood: "Salvation is far from the wicked." As in the previous stanza, he plays with themes of nearness and distance. He said before that the wicked were far from God's law and here he says that these wicked are far from God's salvation.

Yet after the weightiness of these opening verses, the psalmist writes wonderfully comforting words in the next two verses, 156-157, the middle two verses of the stanza. He also shows his poetic skills in doing so. In the ESV, verse 156 reads: "Great is your mercy, O Lord." Yet that does not quite capture what the psalmist means. The psalmist does not say that God's mercy is great, as if God's mercy is one really, really big thing. If he had said that we would nod in agreement. It is theologically correct. But the psalmist's point is that God's mercies are *many*. That is how he speaks in the Hebrew. He does not communicate that God's mercy is one big thing but that God's mercies are so many. The psalmist's words resonate with Lamentations 3. Lamentations is a very dark book overall, but there are some beautifully hopeful, joyous statements in the middle of it. An example is this: God's "mercies never come to an end; they are new every morning." This expresses the idea that God's mercies are *many*. They come in the plural.

You might be wondering why I emphasize this point. The answer is that verse 157 uses the same term again: "many." "*Many* are my persecutors and my adversaries." But the psalmist is prepared for them. However many enemies he faces, God's mercies are as many. This is also true for us, and what a great encouragement that is. Day after day, we have afflictions. Day after day, we face trials. Day after day, enemies oppose us. But for every day that there is trouble, God pours out mercy to help and provide. God's mercies are many.

Two more ideas are worth noting in this Resh stanza. One appears in the next two verses, 158-159. Both verses begin with a Hebrew word for "look" or "see." The ESV has: "I look at the faithless with disgust…. Consider [or "see"] how I love your precepts." The psalmist also used the same word in verse 153, the first of the stanza: "Look on my affliction and deliver me." Three of the eight verses in the stanza begin with the same word, the word for "look." Since this is the Resh stanza, the first word of every verse begins with the letter Resh. As you may have guessed, this word for "look" is a common Hebrew term that begins with this letter. The psalmist capitalizes on this.

In verse 153, the first of these occurrences, and then too in verse 159, the last occurrence, the psalmist asks *God* to see *him*. He wants God to see his affliction and how he loves his precepts. This is worth a moment's reflection. It is remarkable that a human being would want God to see him. You would think that sinners would prefer to stay hidden from the holy God. If you are unreconciled with God and thus still under his judgment, why would you want God to see you? It would be wiser to be like those people on judgment day, in Revelation 6, who will call for the mountains to fall upon them and hide them. But if through trust in Christ you are reconciled with God, then you can ask God to see you and there is nothing to fear. In fact, you *want* God to see you, because that means he will help you. The God who sees knows your troubles and knows that you love and seek him. This is part of Christian prayer. We ask God to see us and know us. We lay bare our hearts before God, as considered earlier.

But notice also, in verse 158, the second of the three occurrences of this word for "look," that the psalmist describes his own seeing. He says: "I look at the faithless with disgust, because they do not keep your commands." This statement might make us a little uncomfortable. Perhaps it strikes us as uncharitable or judgmental. "I look at the faithless with disgust"—is that how we are supposed to look at fellow human beings, even if they are unbelievers? You might think of it in the following way. One of the common temptations we sinners have—even Christian sinners—is that we envy the wicked. We look at wicked people and wish we could be them. They may enjoy certain advantages in life because they do not have the moral scruples we have. They can enjoy certain pleasures that we do not, because they do not fear God. It may be tempting for you who are young to look at non-Christian friends and wish that you could do what they do. Your parents have the same kinds of temptations.

From this perspective, put yourself in the psalmist's shoes. He looks at the faithless with disgust not because he is uncharitable but because a godly person should not find the wicked person's way of life attractive. We should not envy the wicked. We should not want to be able to do what the wicked can do. No, let us pray that God will give us godly hearts that find the ways of wickedness revolting. This is our psalmist. He looks at the faithless with disgust because they do not keep God's commands.

That brings us to the end of our stanza, verse 160: "The sum of your word is truth, and every one of your righteous rules endures forever." That should sound familiar because it is so like the end of the previous stanza. We see again how this psalm fits together and how the psalmist weaves themes together throughout it. What a wonderful way to end the stanza and what a great reminder for us as we conclude.

God's word is true. God's word endures forever. As we look to God day after day and expect God's mercies one day after the next, remember that God ministers his mercy through his word. His word reveals the many mercies of God for you. That revelation of his mercy is true, and it is forever. Neither God's word nor his mercies will ever fail you.

11

The Character of the Godly

Psalm 119:161-176

We might ask ourselves: How do things go for us spiritually when affairs in life go very poorly? Or you might wonder: if I had to live in a place with severe religious oppression, what would be the state of my spiritual health? These questions are worth asking because this is our psalmist's situation. The author of Psalm 119 had an extremely difficult life. He tells us that he has been a rebel against God and that God brought trouble upon him because of that. God made him a sojourner in a foreign land, away from the land of Israel. We also know that the psalmist endured serious oppression. Powerful people persecuted him, even seeking his life. We are tempted to feel sorry for ourselves sometimes, but few if any of us have experienced anything as bad as what our psalmist faced.

As we come to the last two stanzas of Psalm 119, the psalmist has hardly forgotten about his hardships. They have been on his mind throughout this beautiful poem. Yet as he comes to the end of the Long Psalm, he expresses no spirit of bitterness or complaining. Instead, he displays a remarkable spiritual vitality and maturity as he wrestles with his status before God in this world. In describing himself as he does here, our psalmist is not puffing himself up or creating a falsely optimistic picture of his spiritual health. He ends, in fact, on a note of profound humility, acknowledging that there is much he does not know, much that he cannot do, and much that he cannot control. Yet the psalmist devotes himself to God with a profound faith, a faith that has blossomed into a godly character—a godly character well-suited for an old covenant saint living in difficult circumstances but anticipating the great deliverance that God will bring for his people.

* * * * *

We begin with the first of our two stanzas, Sin and Shin, verses 161-168. This stanza begins with a simple statement: "Princes persecute me without cause." The psalmist made similar claims earlier in Psalm 119. He is not simply being hounded by wicked people. He is suffering official persecution. That is, civil authorities are persecuting him. This is probably the most fearful kind of persecution. It is frightening enough when ordinary people oppress believers, but when powerful people do it, that is far more frightening.

Think about this in context. God had promised in the Mosaic law that when his old covenant people Israel sinned, he would send judgment against them. The Lord often brought that judgment by raising up foreign political powers. The historical narratives of the Old Testament speak about the kings of Egypt, Syria, Assyria, and Babylon as instruments of God's judgment against his people. This does not mean, of course, that these foreign rulers acted justly when they overpowered Israel. Often God judged these foreign rulers at a later date for mistreating his people. This is at least part of why our psalmist says that princes persecuted him *without cause*. It is not as if these foreign princes had any just cause against our psalmist. But he was still suffering under them, and God's judgment against his covenant people was in the background.

So that is the opening line—the first half of the first verse of the stanza. What is so remarkable about the rest of the stanza— the remaining fifteen-sixteenths—is that the psalmist does not say a single thing more about this persecution. He expresses no bitterness and does not complain at all. Instead, he reflects entirely upon his spiritual virtues and upon the blessings God has granted.

Before we examine this in detail, we should step back and think for a moment. Many Christians living in the West today are concerned about shifts in the culture and imminent threats of political opposition. Although we have it so much better than the psalmist, many today feel under siege. If we feel this way, what is our response? Do we sit around complaining? Is bitterness growing in our heart? Do we feel that we are losing what is most valuable to us? Or, in contrast, does our response look like the psalmist's? The psalmist shows a godly response to suffering, especially to opposition for the sake of the faith.

We can consider how the psalmist further responds in the verses that follow and begin with the second part of the first verse of this stanza, 161: "But my heart stands in awe of your words." The threat of oppressive civil authorities certainly provokes fear. We might describe it as the *fear of man*. Notice, then, that the psalmist responds to the fear of man by *fearing God*. He stands in awe of God's word. Throughout Scripture, the fear of the Lord and his word is one of the most fundamental virtues of the godly person. The fear of the Lord is not a fear of terror but a fear of respect, awe, and reverence. One of the wonderful things about the fear of God is that it relieves us of the fear of man. If you truly fear God—recognizing that the omnipotent

God is on your side and fighting for you—powerful people will not seem so powerful any longer. The psalmist is in awe of God and his word, and that gives him a strong defense against fear of human persecution.

In verse 162 the psalmist next says: "I rejoice at your word like one who finds great spoil." *Joy* is his next response to his difficult circumstances. We might describe joy as *delight*. Joy in the Lord—the virtue of Christian joy—is delight in the Lord and in all the blessings we have from him. This includes delight in his word, which announces such good news and encouragement. When we are not feeling very joyful in the Lord, it is tempting to think: "Well, if things were going better, if I didn't have so many problems weighing me down, I could certainly be more joyful." But that is exactly the opposite of the way Scripture speaks about joy. In texts such as Romans 5 and James 1, the New Testament calls us to rejoice in our sufferings. In fact, one of the primary ways the Lord builds joy in his people is through affliction, as counterintuitive as that seems. If you think you are joyful when things are going well, you should probe your heart and inquire whether your joy is really in the Lord. Perhaps what you think is Christian joy is only delight in worldly things that provide temporary pleasure or the illusion of success. We really know that our joy is in *the Lord* when he takes away temporal delights. It is a hard lesson for all of us. But let us set our hearts on the Lord, even during times of affliction. This was the psalmist's response to persecution.

The next verse, 163, says: "I hate and abhor falsehood, but I love your law." He turns from joy to love. This is a natural progression because love and joy belong together. Why do we rejoice in God and his law? We do so because we love them. We rejoice in what we love. If you really love a person, you will delight in that person's company and well-being. If you say you love someone and you dislike being with him or her, something is not right. Because we love the Lord and love his word, we rejoice in them. The psalmist rejoices in God because he loves God and his word.

This progression of thought continues in verse 164: "Seven times a day I praise you for your righteous rules." What is the only proper response for those who fear the Lord and his word, rejoice in them, and love them? Worship! Hence the psalmist praises the Lord for his word. This is what we are doing right now. We have come together to worship the Lord. We do this as his people with reverence, love, and delight. Your presence at this divine worship service indicates that you wish to worship, but it is fitting to examine our hearts as we do. Perhaps you fail to find worship encouraging and comforting. If so, that is a spiritual problem to take seriously. Verse 164 suggests that it is symptomatic of a yet deeper problem: of not fearing the Lord and his word as we ought, and of not loving and rejoicing in them as we ought. Pray that the Lord would build that fear and joy and love in you, and that it might flow forth into sincere, heartfelt praise. "Seven times a day," he says, "I praise you." Seven represents perfection in Scripture. We should render all of our praise to God, with all that is in us.

The psalmist is not finished describing his remarkable spiritual state. In verse 165 he continues: "Great peace have those who love your law; nothing can make them stumble." He is really outdoing himself now! Remember, he began this stanza stating that princes were persecuting him. That does not sound very peaceful. Yet the psalmist says that those who love God's law have not only peace, but *great* peace. He obviously is not talking about earthly peace. He did not enjoy peace of that sort at that time. Rather he describes spiritual peace. He is at peace with God. In the past, he was a rebel, but he repented and placed his confidence in God—and he enjoys great peace now.

Nothing can make him stumble. What a remarkable statement for one who has struggled with his devotion to God in the past.

He takes it another step further in the next verse, 166: "I hope for your salvation, O LORD, and I do your commandments." This turns to the virtue of hope. Hope looks to the future. It is a future-oriented character trait. By hope, we have confidence that the Lord will fulfill all his promises to his people. The Lord will not fail to carry out a single thing he has committed himself to do. This is so fitting for the psalmist to mention here. He has great spiritual peace, but he is not at peace in this world. Yet he has hope. We might say that he is content before the Lord, but he is not fully satisfied. He knows that the Lord has promised not merely an inner spiritual peace but also a complete, holistic peace for his people. The Lord will provide peace from all outward oppression. The psalmist looks in hope for the day when he will no longer suffer persecution, when his great peace will extend to every aspect of his life.

As we reach this point in our text, let me call your attention to Romans 5:1-5. In these verses, in the midst of his thorough presentation of Christian salvation in the book of Romans, Paul describes the character of the Christian. These opening verses of Romans 5 are a wonderfully concise depiction of the Christian life. And notice how many of the things Paul says correspond to what we have been considering in Psalm 119. Romans 5 states that those who have been justified by faith have peace with God through our Lord Jesus Christ. That is, all who believe in the Lord Jesus, whose sins are forgiven, and thus whom God has pronounced righteous in Christ, have *peace*. This is not worldly peace, but spiritual peace with God. Paul goes on to say that we *rejoice in our sufferings*. We can rejoice in suffering because we have peace with God as the justified. And then he explains that this suffering in which we rejoice produces endurance, which produces character, which produces *hope*. And this hope will not put us to shame. This new covenant Christian life that Paul presents in Romans 5 sounds remarkably like the response to suffering that our psalmist describes in the Sin and Shin stanza.

As the psalmist reaches the end of this stanza, he speaks of his obedience to God's commands. Verse 166 says: "I do your commandments." Then, both verses 167 and 168 speak of keeping God's testimonies and precepts. The psalmist also says in verse 168 that he does so because all his ways are before God. For sinners, the idea that our ways are before God is not entirely comfortable. Do we really want our ways to be evident before God? Surely, we would prefer to keep many things secret from him. Yet those who trust in the Lord—who know the fear of God and the joy of Christ and who have peace and hope— may walk before God without the need to hide anything from his eyes. This is not because their ways are perfect, but because they know that God is merciful. God is sanctifying them and will continue to conform them to the image of Christ. They pursue the life of obedience before their God, with their ways open before him, in all honesty, knowing that he will continue to do his good work within them.

* * * * *

To our sensibilities, the Sin and Shin stanza would be a perfect way to end Psalm 119. It presents the psalmist at his most spiritually mature, with a Romans 5-type spirituality. But ending here would not provide an accurate picture of his spiritual condition. Psalm 119 is honest. The psalmist is not concerned about public image. He is not going to end the psalm in a way that will make himself look as good as possible.

Therefore, our psalmist proceeds for one last stanza, Taw. Taw reminds us that he is a suffering man. He still bears the scars of his past rebellion and the divine judgment he endured because of it. And he is not at all sure how God will work out all things for his good. He believes that God will, but how?

A pattern emerges in the first half of the stanza, verses 169-172, a pattern which the second half of the stanza will almost repeat. The psalmist offers petitions to God and then praises him. The first two verses, then, are requests. This is worth noting in context. The psalmist has made many requests throughout Psalm 119, but in the previous stanza he did not offer one. Yet this new stanza begins: "Let my cry come before you…. Give me understanding…. Let my plea come before you; deliver me according to your word." As he has done so many times, the psalmist acknowledges his neediness. He needs understanding, for God's ways are still so hard to fathom. He needs deliverance according to God's word, for he still faces persecution.

But even as the psalmist offers these pleas for help, note where he goes in the next verses, 171-172. He returns to the worship of God. Verse 171: "My lips will pour forth praise, for you teach me your statutes." He had said that he wanted understanding, and so here he praises God for being his teacher. Verse 172: "My tongue will sing of your word." One of the important things we do in worship is to burst forth and sing because all God's commands are right. The psalmist establishes a helpful pattern that we do well to follow. When we pray, our instinct is often to pray about ourselves—to ask God to help us, provide for us, and relieve us of our problems. The psalmist does some of this, and we too should seek God's help in our lives. But that is not the heart of prayer. The heart of prayer is praising God. Our prayers should be first of all about *him*, not about us. What a wonderful pattern the psalmist follows. He pleads with God for help but turns those pleas into songs of praise to God.

Four verses remain in the stanza. Since the first four verses followed a pattern of petition and then praise, we might expect something similar in the second half. And we get something close to that. Verse 173 reads: "Let your hand be ready to help me." So again, he offers a petition, asking for God's help. Then in verse 174 he does not exactly petition God for something, but he does again express his need and desire for God's help: "I long for your salvation, O LORD." For the psalmist to continue his pattern, then, the next verse would turn back to praise. And indeed, verse 175 does not disappoint us: "Let my soul live and praise you, and let your rules help me." The psalmist has asked for life so many times in this psalm. Note that he does not ask for his life to be extended for selfish reasons, but for the sake of praising the Lord. How, then, do we expect this psalm to end? We expect high praise for God. How fitting it would be for the psalmist to conclude on an exalted note of worship!

But that is not how it happens. The last verse of the Long Psalm reads: "I have gone astray like a lost sheep; seek your servant, for I do not forget your commandments." It may strike us as anti-climactic. He confesses how weak and helpless he is, asking for God to look for him. He does remember God's commandments, but only as a lost sheep. He does not end on a note of confidence.

I know that this is an awkward way to end the chapter. But in the next chapter we will consider Psalm 119 as a whole and reflect how to read it as new covenant Christians. We will return to the final verse and see how helpfully this ending puts Psalm 119 in its proper place in redemptive history and anticipates the glorious coming of our Lord Jesus Christ.

12

A Shepherd for Sojourners

Psalm 119:1-176

In this chapter, I wish to look with you at Psalm 119 as a whole. Of course, we cannot do that in detail. But one of the challenging aspects of reading and meditating on Psalm 119 is figuring out how this Long Psalm fits together. Surely this psalm is more than 176 individual pious statements collected randomly in one place. So, how is Psalm 119 organized and how do its ideas develop? And what does the psalmist tell us about himself and his spiritual condition? More importantly, what does this psalm teach its readers? What specifically does it teach *us*, who live under the new covenant and study this psalm after the coming of our Lord Jesus Christ?

This final chapter on the Great Psalm suggests some answers to these questions, with the prayer that it may stimulate us all to keep meditating on this psalm all our lives and keep growing in godliness through its profound teaching.

* * * * *

We begin, then, by thinking about the movement of this psalm. Let's take a rapid survey of Psalm 119 from beginning to end and consider how the psalmist develops his thoughts.

Psalm 119 has a grand opening. In the Aleph and Beth stanzas, the psalmist describes clearly how the law of God requires perfect obedience. It demands devotion from the bottom of one's heart. And with only a brief suggestion otherwise, the psalmist portrays himself as wholly committed to God's law. He recognizes its requirement for holistic obedience and strives to offer that devotion to God and his word.

Yet we do not need to read far into Psalm 119 before we learn that matters are a bit more complicated than we may have gathered from the opening stanzas. Already in the third stanza, Gimel, the psalmist reveals that something is very wrong with his life and condition, for he tells us that he is a sojourner on the earth. He is not living comfortably and prosperously in his home, on the plot of ground that God gave to his ancestors long before. He is not enjoying the blessedness that God promised his people if they were obedient and faithful to him. No, he is a sojourner. He is away from the Promised Land and living among pagan Gentiles. He also tells us that he is persecuted by princes and that his soul clings to the dust. To use language from elsewhere in the Old Testament, our psalmist is in exile. He may have been one of the exiles in Babylon, although we cannot be sure. But we do know with certainty that things are not well with the psalmist.

Nevertheless, he portrays himself as obedient to God's law. And thus we confront a puzzle early in Psalm 119: how can it be that this man, who is so committed to God's law, is suffering so terribly, especially when God's law promised blessing to those who obey? We should keep this question in mind as we continue.

The next four stanzas are He, Waw, Zayin, and Heth. The psalmist develops twin themes in these stanzas. On the one hand, he is confident. He is a man of faith, and he trusts that the Lord will deliver him. God has not forgotten him. The psalmist makes many wonderful statements here about the grace of God. On the other hand, he will not let us forget about his dire situation. He keeps returning repeatedly to the fact that he is under persecution and suffering in all sorts of ways. In Zayin, he reminds us that he is a sojourner. He obviously does not want us to forget this. In that same context, he also expresses hot indignation toward the wicked. Furthermore, a couple of times he mentions his nighttime vigils. Throughout Scripture, darkness and night have ominous connotations. Bad things tend to happen at night. Nighttime often represents the sorrow and trials of the soul.

As we read these four stanzas, then, we keep wondering why our psalmist is in this condition. He is a man of faith, committed to God's word, yet he suffers greatly.

The Teth and Yodh stanzas follow. These stanzas provide a theological breakthrough. The psalmist does not answer all our questions here, but he does provide considerable illumination. He finally tells us why he is a sojourner, living in exile: he was a rebel against God. Thus far he has spoken at length about his commitment to God and his law, but now he tells us—in verse 67 for the first time—that before he was afflicted, he went astray. The psalmist was not always devoted to God's word. These stanzas teach us both that he was a rebel against God and that God had afflicted him. His affliction was punishment, God's judgment for his rebellion. In fact, this is exactly what should have happened, given what God's law teaches. Psalm 119 speaks much about God's law, and God's Old Testament law told the Israelites that, if they rebelled against him, he would punish them. The greatest punishment he threatened was exile from their land.

The psalmist, however, also tells us something very encouraging in these stanzas. He reports that he has repented. He learned from his hardships and turned back to his God. And God had restored him—if not in his outward condition, at least inwardly and spiritually. Not only that, but he also reports that other Israelites, his countrymen, have been encouraged through him. Verse 74: "Those who fear you shall see me and rejoice, because I have hoped in your word." Then again in verse 79: "Let those who fear you turn to me, that they may know your testimonies." His example of repentance and restoration has lifted the spirits of others.

After this turning point in Psalm 119, we might expect the psalmist's mood to remain very upbeat. But that is certainly not the case. The next stanza, Kaph, is the darkest stanza of the entire psalm. He writes its sobering words as he approaches the halfway point, since Kaph is the final stanza of the first half of the psalm—the eleventh of twenty-two. In Kaph the psalmist tells us, for example, that he is like a wineskin in the smoke. Whatever exactly that is, it is not something you want to be! The psalmist says almost nothing positive about his condition in the Kaph stanza. He only emphasizes how bitterly he is suffering.

But then we come to the halfway point of the psalm—we make the turn, to use a golf metaphor—and perhaps the two most positive stanzas in Psalm 119 greet us. This is surely one of the most dramatic U-turns in Scripture. In the Lamed and Mem stanzas, and even through the beginning of the Nun stanza, we find some of the most exalted, as well as some of the most familiar, statements in Psalm 119. The psalmist tells us that God's word is fixed and established in the heavens. It cannot be moved. He reminds us that God's word is true and profound. All perfection has a limit, he says at the end of Lamed, but he has not seen any limits to God's word. It is "exceedingly broad." Then, in Mem, he declares his love for God's law and how God's law imparts wisdom and understanding. At the beginning of Nun he adds that God's word is a lamp to his feet and a light to his path.

We may wonder why the psalmist says these wonderful, beautiful things about God's word *here*, early in the second part of Psalm 119. Of course, all he says is true of God's word in general. But the psalmist may emphasize such things at this point because of some insight he attained through the law that he had not really understood previously. The psalmist had surely been taught God's law from an early age. But when he wrote in earlier stanzas about his rebellion and subsequent punishment, he stated that it was good to be afflicted and that he had learned God's statutes through that experience of affliction, repentance, and restoration. What was he referring to? To answer this, it may be helpful to remember that "the law," for the ancient Hebrews, often referred to the first five books of the Old Testament. One of the things the psalmist had opportunity to learn from his suffering and repentance, then, was that God's "law"—Genesis through Deuteronomy—not only gave many commands telling Israel what to do but also made many promises of grace to sinners. In those books of the law, God told Israel that if they disobeyed him and he exiled them far from their land, he would also restore them. He would bring them back. God promised to renew his grace to his sinful, rebellious people. The psalmist's experience had provided occasion to reflect on these matters. He had surely come to appreciate and revel in the full message of God's word as he never had before.

Psalm 119 has covered a great deal of ground thus far, but the psalmist still has many stanzas to go. In the Samekh and

Ayin stanzas, he reflects on the judgment of God. He focuses not on God's judgment against Israel but against the wicked. The psalmist calls God to judge their enemies. This is part of the salvation of God's people. As Scripture often communicates, for God's people to be saved, their enemies must be judged. The psalmist was so zealous for this that in verse 126 he informs God that it is time for him to act. He tells God that he needs to get to work, judging their enemies and saving his people. Their restoration depends upon this.

Then, in the follow stanzas—Pe, Tsadhe, Qoph, and Resh— the psalmist continues to look forward to God's full restoration of his people from their state of exile and oppression. In Pe and Tsadhe, our psalmist identifies certain feelings or emotions he is experiencing. He speaks about his longing for God and his word, about his deep sorrow for his sins and the sins of his people, and about his zeal—his zeal especially for the display of God's righteousness in a broken and unrighteous world. Then in Qoph, and continuing into Resh, the psalmist discusses prayer. The psalmist is a man of prayer as he waits for God's deliverance of his people. He lifts his voice to God continually, day and night, asking God to be near and to deliver him from his enemies.

As he reaches the final two stanzas, the psalmist radiates a state of spiritual maturity. He suffers so terribly and has waited so long for God to rescue his people that we might expect him to be bitter. Yet no bitterness weighs him down. Instead, in Sin and Shin, he expresses fear, joy, love, praise, and hope in God and his word. And in the final stanza, Taw, he follows a pattern of petition followed by praise. In the first two verses he makes requests and then he offers praise in the next two verses. The same pattern seems to emerge in the next verses: in verses 173- 174 he tells God of his needs and then in verse 175 he praises him. The psalmist sets us up for a grand finale. We expect

Psalm 119 to end with a majestic expression of praise to God. It would fit the pattern of the stanza. But that is not what the author does. He ends anti-climactically on a down note. Verse 176: "I have gone astray like a lost sheep; seek your servant, for I do not forget your commandments."

It is a striking and unexpected way for the psalmist to end. What does he intend to communicate? Has he fallen again? Has he rebelled against God as he did previously? That seems unlikely in the context since the previous stanza radiated such spiritual maturity. We might ask instead if the psalmist is merely confessing that he is a sinner. We are all sinners as long as we are in this life, after all. Is verse 176 simply a way to express that?

Probably not. Several Old Testament texts use imagery like what we find in this last verse of Psalm 119—that is, imagery of going astray, being a lost sheep, and needing a shepherd. In light of these other Old Testament texts, as well as the context of Psalm 119, the psalmist's final verse is communicating, one last time, that he is a sojourner. He is in exile rather than enjoying the blessing of God in the Promised Land. He and his compatriots are scattered like lost sheep.

Think about a few of these other Old Testament texts for a moment. Psalm 80 calls on God as the Shepherd of Israel. It calls on him to lead them like a flock. God needed to stir up his might, save them, and restore them. That sounds similar to Psalm 119. Psalm 80 also acknowledges that God has been angry with his people's prayers. He had given them over to their enemies. God had broken down Israel's walls. God had judged his people. Again, we can see the similarities to Psalm 119. What does Psalm 80 ask of God in response to his wrath? It asks God to put his hand on the man of his right hand, the "son of man" he made strong for himself. The psalmist looks for this son of man to come and deliver his people. That is, they needed a great Savior whom God the Shepherd would appoint to deliver them from their state of exile.

Or consider Ezekiel 34. Ezekiel prophesied during the early days of the Babylonian exile. In Ezekiel 34, God condemned the human shepherds of Israel, such as their kings and other leaders. These human shepherds had harmed the flock rather than helped it. The flock was full of the sick, the injured, the strays, and the lost. Again, some of the same imagery is at the end of Psalm 119. What did God say in Ezekiel 34 in response? He promised that he himself would come and seek his people, search for the lost and stray sheep, and gather them from the countries in which they are scattered. God himself would come, shepherd his people, and thereby rescue them from exile.

Think about one other Old Testament text: Isaiah 40:11. Isaiah wrote before the exile in Babylon, but he prophesied about it. In Isaiah 40, he prophesied that God would deliver his people from exile. Note how Isaiah described this divine deliverance. Isaiah 40:11 says that God would tend his flock like a shepherd on their return to their land. He would gather the lambs in his arms and carry them in his bosom. He would gently lead those with young. This promises that God would do exactly what our psalmist sought at the end of Psalm 119: that God would gather his people from exile and shepherd his beleaguered sheep scattered among the nations.

How can we not turn to the New Testament as well? As John 10 especially testifies, Christ the Good Shepherd is the answer to the psalmist's plea. In a way, it is obvious to anyone who has read the New Testament. Christ has come. God promised of old that he himself would shepherd his people and that a son of man would accomplish this work. Christ, both Son of God and son of man, is the one and only fulfillment of these great promises. He has laid down his life for his people. He has gathered his sheep and continues to gather them—not only the ones close by but also those far away, not only Jews but also Gentiles.

As we consider the end of Psalm 119, then, it is important to recognize that we who live under the new covenant are *not* wandering sheep in the way our psalmist was. Christ has purchased us. He has welcomed us into his sheepfold. If you are a baptized member of Christ's church, you were welcomed into the sheepfold of the Lord Jesus Christ. You are members of that fold already. You are citizens of heaven, the New Testament now tells us. You are heirs of the restored heavenly Promised Land, heirs of a kingdom that cannot be shaken. You who trust in Christ, members of his church, have already been sought and found. Christ has brought you in. The psalmist asked God to act in a way that he has now acted in Christ.

Please also note that the New Testament does not describe the church as wandering sheep, as the Old Testament repeatedly described the old covenant people. As the apostle Peter put it at the end of 1 Peter 2: "You *were* straying like sheep, but have *now* returned to the Shepherd and Overseer of your souls." What a blessing this is! There is much we still do not understand, of course, much that is still puzzling and troubling about our lives in this world. But we know so much more than the psalmist of God's saving work, and we enjoy blessings far beyond what our old covenant spiritual ancestors enjoyed.

Yet, 1 Peter 2 also says that we new covenant people are sojourners and exiles. Why? Because we are not in heaven. We have been sought and found, and made members of the sheepfold of Christ, but we are not in glory yet. Thus, life is still full of trials and temptations. This is why much of Psalm 119 strikes so close to home for us as the psalmist recounts his various afflictions. And we certainly can be *tempted* to wander from the sheepfold. Sometimes we see our fellow church members wander. We see people whom we counted as brothers and sisters leave the fold. Some have denied Christ. It breaks our hearts. There is one place in the New Testament, Matthew 18, which speaks about sheep wandering from God's fold. There Jesus told a parable about a shepherd who has a hundred sheep and one of them wanders off. But what happens? The shepherd goes after it. That shepherd does not wave goodbye, but he pursues that sheep. And the very next text in Matthew 18 tells us *how* Jesus is pleased to pursue wandering sheep in this present age. He does it through his church and through the keys of the kingdom he has entrusted to it. The church, on behalf of Christ, speaks a word of repentance, reconciliation, and restoration to those who wander off.

Do not wander away. Do not leave the sheepfold. Do not leave Christ's church, where he has so graciously gathered you. Perhaps you are tempted to do so. Perhaps in your heart you have already forsaken Christ, even though you are sitting here today. Perhaps someday you will leave the church. If you do, and by God's grace you remember these words, and if Christ through his church calls you back: listen to his word! Listen to his gracious word! Why separate yourself from the flock? Why wander in a hostile, barren land where there is no water? Return to Christ!

And so we come to the end of this psalm. Know that you are so blessed as Christ's sheep—as the redeemed, gathered, sought, and found sheep of the Lord Jesus Christ. Receive the nourishment of your shepherd who loves you, cares for you, and has laid down his life for you. He alone provides true rest and satisfaction.

Also available from Christian Focus Publications ...

MICHAEL LEFEBVRE

SINGING THE SONGS OF JESUS

REVISITING THE PSALMS

978-1-84550-600-1

Singing the Songs of Jesus
Revisiting the Psalms

Michael Lefebvre

The Psalms were composed for singing. In Old and New Testament times, and throughout Church history, congregations sang Psalms. Despite renewed interest in Psalmody, few books explain how the Psalms function as hymns for Christ-centred worship. Singing the Songs of Jesus fills that gap without shying away from difficulties, like the doubts and curses of the Psalms. This study shows why the Psalms are suited for Christian praise and how to use them for powerful and relevant worship.

This book should admirably fulfil the author's purpose by forcing those who have rejected or neglected the psalms in their praise to think again ... If you have never sung the psalms and would like good biblical rather than historical reasons for doing so, and, crucially, if you want the key to understanding what you sing, you should really read this book.

Kenneth Stewart,
Minister, Stornoway Reformed Presbyterian Church,
Stornoway, Isle of Lewis

PHILIP S. ROSS

ANTHEMS
for a DYING
LAMB

How Six Psalms (113–118)
Became a Songbook for the Last Supper
and the Age to Come

978-1-84550-600-1

Anthems for a Dying Lamb

How Six Psalms (113–118) Became a Songbook for the Last Supper and the Age to Come

Philip S. Ross

Anthems for a Dying Lamb offers an in-depth exposition of Psalms 113–118. Often called the Hallel, these psalms were part of the Passover seder, which directed proceedings during the Passover meal. That's one reason the Hallel became known as the 'hymn' that Jesus sang with his disciples at the Last Supper, and why it is often part of communion services when the church celebrates the Lord's Supper. Philip Ross explains Psalms 113–118 in their Old Testament context and shows how the 'trouble and sorrow' of Psalm 116, or the 'cornerstone' of Psalm 118, give us insight into Jesus' ministry and mindset in the hours before his crucifixion.

Don't rush through this book; it should be savored bit by bit. You can bask in its fresh insights, squirm under its searching exposure – and all the while Dr Ross keeps you firmly tethered to Jesus. Here is a mind-filling, soul-nourishing, Christ-focused feast!

Dale Ralph Davis
Author and Old Testament Scholar

Christian Focus Publications

Our mission statement
Staying Faithful

In dependence upon God we seek to impact the world through literature faithful to His infallible Word, the Bible. Our aim is to ensure that the Lord Jesus Christ is presented as the only hope to obtain forgiveness of sin, live a useful life and look forward to heaven with Him.

Our Books are published in four imprints:

◁◻╳ CHRISTIAN FOCUS

Popular works including biographies, commentaries, basic doctrine and Christian living.

◁◻╳ MENTOR

Books written at a level suitable for Bible College and seminary students, pastors, and other serious readers. The imprint includes commentaries, doctrinal studies, examination of current issues and church history.

◁◻╳ CHRISTIAN HERITAGE

Books representing some of the best material from the rich heritage of the church.

◁◻╳ CF4KIDS

Children's books for quality Bible teaching and for all age groups: Sunday school curriculum, puzzle and activity books; personal and family devotional titles, biographies and inspirational stories – because you are never too young to know Jesus!

Christian Focus Publications Ltd,
Geanies House, Fearn, Ross-shire,
IV20 1TW, Scotland, United Kingdom.
www.christianfocus.com